PURPLE HIBISCUS

Chimamanda Ngozi Adichie

AUTHORED by Christine McKeever
UPDATED AND REVISED by Elizabeth Weinbloom

COVER DESIGN by Table XI Partners LLC
COVER PHOTO by Olivia Verma and © 2005 GradeSaver, LLC

BOOK DESIGN by Table XI Partners LLC

Published by GradeSaver LLC, www.gradesaver.com

First published in the United States of America by GradeSaver LLC. 2012

GRADESAVER, the GradeSaver logo and the phrase "Getting you the grade
since 1999" are registered trademarks of GradeSaver, LLC

ISBN 978-1-60259-294-0

Printed in the United States of America

For other products and additional information please visit
http://www.gradesaver.com

Table of Contents

Table of Contents

Biography of Adichie, Chimamanda Ngozi (1977-)

Chimamanda Ngozi Adichie was born September 15, 1977 in Enugu, Nigeria. She was raised in Nsukka near the University of Nigeria. Her father, James Nwoye Adichie, was a professor of statistics and later became the Deputy Vice-Chancellor of the University. Her mother, Ifeoma Aidichie, became the first female registrar at the University. Adichie is the fifth child in a family of six children. She is of Igbo descent and her ancestral home is in Abba.

Adichie was an A student who often butted heads with her teachers. Despite her reputation, she received several academic awards. Adichie enrolled in medical school at the behest of her father. She soon dropped out to pursue her dream of becoming a writer. When she was 19, she left Nigeria on a scholarship to Drexel University in Philadelphia. She studied communication at Drexel and earned a degree in communication and political science at Eastern Connecticut State University. She graduated summa cum laude in 2001. Later that year, she began MFA courses in literature at Johns Hopkins University.

Adichie credits Chinua Achebe, Igbo author of Nigerian masterwork *Things Fall Apart*, with her literary success. She once lived in Achebe's house and believes his halo surrounded her. After reading his book at 10 years old, she realized that people who looked like her could exist in books. Her desire to write was sparked by his work.

In 2003, Purple Hibiscus was published to wide acclaim. It was shortlisted for the Orange Prize and awarded the Commonwealth Writers' Prize for Best First Book. She was awarded with the Orange Prize in 2007 for her second novel, Half of a Yellow Sun, about the Biafran War. In 2008, she received a MacArthur Fellowship. A collection of short stories, The Thing Around Your Neck, was published in 2009.

Adichie tries to combat the image of Africans as portrayed by Western media. Choosing to write first from her experience as an affluent and educated Nigerian, she was often criticized for shying away from the "real" Africa. But she struggled to write characters who were not "starving, or begin bullied by [Zimbabwean dictator] Mugabe, or dying of AIDS." As reflected in her writing voice, Adichie is a staunch feminist and uses her work as a way to work through the misogyny and condescension she has faced as an African woman in the global literary community.

She splits her time between the Unites States and Nigeria, married to a Maryland-based doctor. Her next novel will chronicle the Nigerian immigrant experience in America.

About Purple Hibiscus

Chimamanda Ngozi Adichie's first novel, *Purple Hibiscus*, was widely acclaimed when it was published in 2003. Shortlisted for and awarded several prestigious prizes, *Purple Hibiscus* was praised for capturing a character and a nation on the cusp of radical change. Adichie uses her own childhood experiences to inform the lives of her characters. She was born in Kambili's home town of Enugu, raised in Aunty Ifeoma's university environment in Nsukka, is of Igbo descent, and is a Catholic.

Purple Hibiscus is a story of the corruption and religious fundamentalism that grips Adichie's native country. Told from the point of view of a child, overt political messages are held at an arm's length, but they inform Kambili's coming of age. The wave of bloody coups and corrupt military rule that comprises Nigerian politics are touched upon in the novel through certain characters. Though Papa can be viewed as a metaphor for the dangers of fundamentalism, he tries to put his power to good use by raising social consciousness. Adichie modeled the character Ade Coker after Dele Giwa, a journalist and outspoken critic of the Nigerian government. Giwa was killed by a mail bomb in his home in 1986. Adichie echoes real political activism and events in her novel.

Adichie was a good student in school but, unlike Kambili, she had a reputation for butting heads with her teachers; Obiora is more like Adichie. Purple Hibiscus is a coming of age story for both Kambili and Jaja. While Jaja is not allowed to participate in the Igbo ritual of initiation, both children are able to take considerable steps towards their own adult identities throughout the novel. Inspired by her outspoken aunt and cousin Amaka, Kambili in particular learns to use her voice. Adichie uses Purple Hibiscus to give a voice to African experience that is not typically presented by Western media.

Character List

Kambili Achike

The main character who narrates the story of her family's disintegration. When the story begins, Kambili is fifteen years old and painfully shy. She lives under the strict Catholic rule of her father, who expects his children to succeed at all costs. As political unrest seizes Nigeria, Kambili is introduced to a new way of life by her liberal aunt. Though she retains her faith through several horrendous events, Kambili learns to question authority when necessary.

Jaja (Chukwuka Achike)

Kambili's brother, who is about two years older than her. Like Kambili, Jaja strains under the tyranny of his father. After both his sister and mother are hospitalized from beatings, Jaja begins to rebel. Jaja is rational and protective and more outgoing than his sister. He severs ties with both his father and faith. Jaja takes the blame for his mother's crime.

Papa (Eugene Achike)

A prominent man in the Achike's village of Enugu, Papa runs several successful factories and publishes an English-language newspaper infamous for its criticism of Nigeria's corrupt government. He is a devout Catholic who expects nothing less than perfection from his family. Papa punishes his wife and children in order to correct their behavior. Papa is beloved in his community but is estranged from his own father and his traditional African culture.

Mama (Beatrice Achike)

Mama is a quiet and religious woman, accustomed to obeying the rule of her husband. Though the abuse worsens over time, she refuses to leave. Ultimately, she realizes she must protect her children and poisons her husband.

Aunty Ifeoma

Papa's sister who teaches at the University in nearby Nsukka. Ifeoma is widowed, caring for three children on a meager salary. She is liberal and outspoken but also a devout Catholic. Unlike her brother, she respects the religion and traditions of her father. Her way of life inspires Kambili and Jaja to rethink their own upbringing.

Papa-Nnukwu

Ifeoma and Eugene's father. Papa-Nnukwu is a traditionalist, holding on to the faith of his ancestors. Kambili grows to love Papa-Nnukuw despite her father's warnings that he is a heathen. Through his joy and warm spirit, Kambili learns that both family and faith are more complicated than what she has been taught.

Amaka

Aunty Ifeoma's eldest daughter, fifteen years old. She is fiercely loyal to her Nigerian roots despite her Catholic upbringing. Amaka is critical of her cousin's wealth and meekness. Overtime, Amaka and Kambili come to understand one another and a sisterly bond is forged through adversity.

Obiora

Aunty Ifeoma's eldest son, fourteen years old. Since the death of his father, Obiora has assumed the role of man of the house. He is questioning and mature and delights in intellectual debate. Obiora inspires Jaja to open his eyes.

Chima

Aunty Ifeoma's youngest boy, seven years old. Chima is the baby and does not yet have many responsibilites. He clings onto his mother and to both Obiora and Father Amadi. It is clear he misses a male role model.

Father Amadi

A young missionary priest based in the chaplaincy in Nsukka. Kambili falls in love with him. He is warm and gentle to the children of the village, representing a modern take on faith. He is respectful of his Nigerian roots, incorporating native Igbo songs of worship into his sermons. His bond with Aunty Ifeoma's family is strong. He enjoys lively debate with both Amaka and Obiora. He is taken with Kambili in part because she is so quiet. He encourages Kambili to spread her wings.

Father Benedict

The white, British-born head of St. Agnes, the Achike's church. He is a supportive ally of Papa's, praising him constantly as one of the pillars of the community. Father Benedict is austere and offers only his view of religion.

Ade Coker

The editor of the Standard, Papa's paper. With Papa's support, he is openly critical of the corrupt government and becomes a political target. He is killed by a letter bomb bearing the State Seal.

Yewande Coker

Ade's wife. She is widowed with two young children, who Papa tries to help.

Sisi

The passive servant girl in the Achike household. Sisi provides Mama with the poison used to kill Papa.

Chinwe Yideze

A gossipy classmate of Kambili's. She beats Kambili for head of class in one term.

Ezinne

The only classmate who is kind to Kambili.

Kevin

The Achikes' driver. Mama fires him after Papa dies.

Chiaku

A professor friend of Aunty Ifeoma's, who is critical of a move to America.

Major Themes

Coming of Age

Kambili and Jaja both come of age in *Purple Hibiscus* as a result of their experiences. The book opens with Jaja rebelling against his devout Catholic father by skipping communion on Palm Sunday, an important religious holiday. The following chapters detail the events that culminate in Jaja's defiance. The book is narrated by Kambili three years after this incident. Since she has been stunted by the severe punishments of her father, Kambili barely speaks. Her narration is striking because it can be concluded that she finds her own voice throughout this ordeal. Both Kambili and Jaja take steps towards adulthood by overcoming adversity and being exposed to new thoughts.

Part of growing up is building your own identity by choosing which paths to follow. In Enugu, the only path Kambili and Jaja are allowed to follow is Papa. He writes out schedules and severely punishes them when they stray. When Kambili and Jaja visit their Aunty Ifeoma in Nsukka, they are astonished by what they find. Though her home is small and devoid of luxuries, there is love and respect. Her children Amaka and Obiora are allowed to question authority and choose their own paths. Obiora, though he is three years younger than Jaja, is articulate and protective. He has been initiated into Igbo culture by performing a rite of manhood. Jaja was not allowed to participate and is ashamed that he is lagging behind his cousin. In Nsukka, Jaja is encouraged to rethink his allegiances and make his own decisions.

Aunty Ifeoma encourages Kambili to reconsider her stance on Papa-Nnukwu. As she has been taught by Papa, her grandfather is a heathen. But when she searches his face, she sees no signs of godliness. After witnessing his innocence ritual, Kambili questions the absolute rule of her father. Both Kambili and Jaja take major steps towards adulthood by claiming their individuality.

Religion

There is a contrast between Father Benedict and Father Amadi. Priest at Papa's beloved St. Agnes, Father Benedict is a white man from England who conducts his masses according to European custom. Papa adheres to Father Benedict's style, banishing every trace of his own Nigerian heritage. Papa uses his faith to justify abusing his children. Religion alone is not to blame. Papa represents the wave of fundamentalism in Nigeria that corrupts faith.

Father Amadi, on the other hand, is an African priest who blends Catholicism with Igbo traditions. He believes that faith is both simpler and more complex than what Father Benedict preaches. Father Amadi is a modern African man who is culturally-conscious but influenced by the colonial history of his country. He is not a moral absolutist like Papa and his God. Religion, when wielded by someone gentle, can be a positive force, as it is in Kambili's life.

Papa-Nnukwu is a traditionalist. He follows the rituals of his ancestors and believes in a pantheistic model of religion. Though both his son and daughter converted to Catholicism, Papa-Nnukwu held on to his roots. When Kambili witnesses his morning ritual, she realizes that their faiths are not as different as they appear. Kambili's faith extends beyond the boundaries of one religion. She revels in the beauty of nature, her family, her prayer, and the Bible. When she witnesses the miracle at Aokpe, Kambili's devotion is confirmed. Aunty Ifeoma agrees that God was present even though she did not see the apparition. God is all around Kambili and her family, and can take the form of a smile.

The individualistic nature of faith is explored in Purple Hibiscus. Kambili tempers her devotion with a reverence for her ancestors. Jaja and Amaka end up rejecting their faith because it is inexorably linked to Papa and colonialism, respectively.

Colonialism

Colonialism is a complex topic in Nigeria. For Papa-Nnukwu, colonialism is an evil force that enslaved the Igbo people and eradicated his traditions. For Papa, colonialism is responsible for his access to higher education and grace. For Father Amadi, it has resulted in his faith but he sees no reason that the old and new ways can't coexist. Father Amadi represents modern Nigeria in the global world.

Papa is a product of a colonialist education. He was schooled by missionaries and studied in English. The wisdom he takes back to Nigeria is largely informed by those who have colonized his country. He abandons the traditions of his ancestors and chooses to speak primarily in British-accented English in public. His large estate is filled with western luxuries like satellite TV and music. Amaka assumes that Kambili follows American pop stars while she listens to musicians who embrace their African heritage. But the trappings of Papa's success are hollow. The children are not allowed to watch television. His home, modernized up to Western standards, is for appearances only. There is emptiness in his home just as his accent is falsified in front of whites.

Over the course of the novel, both Kambili and Jaja must come to terms with the lingering after-effects of colonialism in their own lives. They both adjust to life outside their father's grasp by embracing or accepting traditional ways.

Nigerian Politics

Both Kambili and the nation are on the cusp of dramatic changes. The political climate of Nigeria and the internal drama of the Achike family are intertwined. After Nigeria declared independence from Britain in 1960, a cycle of violent coups and military dictatorship led to civil war, which led to a new cycle of bloody unrest. Even democracy is hindered by the wide-spread corruption in the government.

In *Purple Hibiscus*, there is a coup that culminates in military rule. Papa and his paper, the Standard, are critical of the corruption that is ushered in by a leader who is not elected by the people. Ironically, Papa is a self-righteous dictator in his own home. He is wrathful towards his children when they stray from his chosen path for them. In the wake of Ade Coker's death, Papa beats Kambili so severely she is hospitalized in critical condition. Both in Nigeria and in the home, violence begets violence.

Kambili and Jaja are kept away from the unrest at first. They witness protests, deadly roadblocks, and harassment from the safety of their car. But when they arrive in Nsukka, they are thrust into political debate. Obiora says the university is a microcosm for Nigeria – ruled by one man with all the power. Pay has been withheld from the professors and light and power are shut off frequently. Medical workers and technicians go on strike and food prices rise. There are rumors that the sole administrator is misdirecting funds intended for the university. This is a parallel to what is happening in the country at large. Kambili and Jaja now understand firsthand the struggle of their cousins. The personal becomes political, and vice versa.

Silence

Several characters are gripped with silence throughout the novel. Kambili suffers the most, unable to speak more than rehearsed platitudes without stuttering or coughing. Her silence is a product of the abuse that she endures at the hands of her father. Kambili does not allow herself to tell the truth about her situation at home. When her classmates taunt her for being a backyard snob, she does not explain that she does not socialize out of fear. She is not allowed to dally after school lest she be late and beaten. She finally learns how to speak her mind when she is taunted continuously be her cousin Amaka. Aunty Ifeoma encourages her to defend herself and only then can Amaka and Kambili begin their friendship. Kambili begins to speak more confidently, laugh and even sing.

The titles of the second and fourth section are Speaking With Our Spirits and A Different Silence. Kambili and Jaja communicate through their eyes, not able to utter the ugly truth of their situation. Mama, like her daughter, cannot speak freely in her own home. Only with Aunty Ifeoma can she behave authentically. The silence that falls upon Enugu after Papa is murdered is, as the title suggests, different. There is hopelessness to this silence like the one that existed when Papa was alive. But it is an honest silence. Mama and Kambili know the truth and there is nothing more that can be said. Jaja's silence betrays a hardness that has taken hold of him in prison. There is nothing he can say that will end the torment he experiences. The tapes that Aunty Ifeoma sends with her children's voices are the only respite he has.

Silence is also used as punishment. When Kambili and Jaja arrive in Nsukka for Easter, Jaja refuses to speak to his father when he calls. After the years of silence that he has imposed upon his children, they use it as a weapon against him. The government also silences Ade Coker by murdering him after he prints a damning story in the Standard. When soldiers raid Aunty Ifeoma's flat, they are trying to silence her sympathies with the rioting students through intimidation. Silence is a type of violence.

Domestic Violence

On several occasions, Papa beats his wife and children. Each time, he is provoked by an action that he deems immoral. When Mama does not want to visit with Father Benedict because she is ill, Papa beats her and she miscarries. When Kambili and Jaja share a home with a heathen, boiling water is poured on their feet because they have walked in sin. For owning a painting of Papa-Nnukwu, Kambili is kicked until she is hospitalized.

Papa rationalizes the violence he inflicts on his family, saying it is for their own good. The beatings have rendered his children mute. Kambili and Jaja are both wise beyond their years and also not allowed to reach adulthood, as maturity often comes with questioning authority. When Ade Coker jokes that his children are too quiet, Papa does not laugh. They have a fear of God. Really, Kambili and Jaja are afraid of their father. Beating them has the opposite effect. They choose the right path because they are afraid of the repercussions. They are not encouraged to grow and to succeed, only threatened with failure when they do not. This takes a toll on Jaja especially, who is ashamed that he is so far behind Obiora in both intelligence and protecting his family. He ends up equating religion with punishment and rejects his faith.

There is an underlying sexism at work in the abuse. When Mama tells Kambili she is pregnant, she mentions that she miscarried several times after Kambili was born. Within the narrative of the novel, Mama loses two pregnancies at Papa's hands. The other miscarriages may have been caused by these beatings as well. When she miscarries, Papa makes the children say special novenas for their mother's forgiveness. Even though he is to blame, he insinuates it is Mama's fault. Mama believes that she cannot exist outside of her marriage. She dismisses Aunty Ifeoma's ideas that life begins after marriage as "university talk." Mama has not been liberated and withstands the abuse because she believes it is just. Ultimately, she poisons Papa because she can see no other way out. The abuse has repressed her to the point that she must resort to murder to escape.

Nature/Environment

The book's namesake flower is a representation of freedom and hope. Jaja is drawn to the unusual purple hibiscus, bred by a botanist friend of Aunty Ifeoma. Aunty Ifeoma has created something new by bringing the natural world together with intelligence. For Jaja, the flower is hope that something new can be created. He longs to break free of his Papa's rule. He takes a stalk of the purple hibiscus home with him, and plants it in their garden. He also takes home the insight he learns from Nsukka. As both blossom, so too do Jaja and his rebellion.

Kambili's shifting attitudes toward nature signify her stage of transformation. During one of the first times she showers at Nsukka, Kambili finds an earthworm in the tub. Rather than coexisting with it, she removes it to the toilet. When Father Amadi takes her to have her hair plaited, she watches a determined snail repeatedly crawl out of a basket. She identifies with the snail as she has tried to crawl out of Enugu and her fate. Later, when she bathes with water scented with the sky, she leaves the worm alone. She acknowledges that God can be found anywhere and she appreciates its determination.

In the opening of the book, Kambili daydreams while looking at the several fruit and flower trees in her yard. This same yard, a signifier of wealth, leaves her open for taunts of "snob" at school. But here she fixates on the beauty of the trees. When she returns from Nsukka after her mother has miscarried, Kambili is sickened by the rotting tree fruit. The rot symbolizes the sickness in the Achike household but also that Kambili is seeing her home with new eyes. Like the trees, she is trapped behind tall walls.

Weather also plays a role in the novel. When Ade Coker dies, there are heavy rains. After Palm Sunday, a violent wind uproots several trees and makes the satellite dish crash to the ground. Rain and wind reflect the drama that unfolds in the Achikes' lives. Mama tells Kambili that a mixture of rain and sun is God's indecision on what to bring. Just as there can be both rain and sun at the same time, there are good and evil intertwined. In nature, Kambili gleans that there are no absolutes. Papa is neither all good or all bad, her faith does not have to be either Catholic or traditionalist, and she can challenge her parents while still being a good child.

Glossary of Terms

Aku
Winged termites

Allamanda
A flowering shrub

Atilogwu
A spirited dance traditional to the Igbo people

Étagère
A shelf that holds small decorative objects

Boubou
A flowing, wide-sleeved robe

Bournvita
A malted drink

Cassava
A root vegetable, also called yuca

Chaplaincy
The institute for missionary clergy

Chin chin
A fried snack similar to a donut

Cocoyam
A root vegetable, also called taro

Confirmation
A rite of initiation similar to a coming of age ceremony in Christianity. Teenage boys and girls choose the name of a saint to adopt as their own in addition to their given name.

Dogonyaro
A big, strong evergreen tree

Enugu

Capital city of Enugu state in Nigeria

Extreme unction

Also known as Anointing of the Sick, a blessing with oils performed for the gravely ill.

Fela

Fela Kuti, a prominent Nigerian musician and political activist who was jailed several times for the critical overtones of his music. The creator of Afrobeat, a musical genre blending jazz and funk with traditional African rhythms.

Frangipani

A flowering tree with fragrant blooms

Fufu

A paste made from boiled starchy root vegetables. Fufu is often molded piece by piece into a utensil for soup and then eaten.

Garri

A grain or porridge made from the grain that is produced from the fermented mash of a cassava

Gmelina

A flowering tree with yellow fruit

Harmattan

A dry and duty wind

Hausa

An ethnic group indigenous to northern Africa, or the language spoken by the Hausa people

Highlife

A musical genre popular in Western Africa characterized by jazzy horns and guitar

Igbo

An ethnic group indigenous to southeastern Nigeria, or the language spoken by the Igbo people

Igwe

A royal figure in the village

Ixora

a flowering shrub, similar to jasmine

Malleable

Capable of being shaped by outside forces, pliable

Missal

A book containing instructions and texts for the celebration of Mass throughout the year

Mmuo

Masquerading spirits represented by a parade of masked men. They offer tributes to their ancestral spirits.

Moi moi

Steamed bean pudding

Naira

Currency in Nigeria

NEPA

National Electric Power Authority, organization that regulates power usage

Ninth Mile

An intersection of three major roads near Enugu

Novena

A devotion consisting of a prayer repeated on nine successive days, asking to obtain special graces

Nzu

Clay

Oblate

A person who is specifically dedicated to God

Okpa

Steamed pea paste

Onyeka

Onyeka Onwenu, a Nigerian singer, actress and politician

Osadebe

Chief Stephen Osita Osadebe, a popular Igbo highlife musician

Panadol

Acetaminaphen, a painkiller

Rosary

A series of prayers in traditional Catholic devotion. A rosary also refers to a strand consisting of a bead for every prayer recited in this series.

Soutane

Cassock, an ankle-length robe worn by clergy

Umunna

The extended family of one's ancestral village

Wrapper

An often colorful piece of cloth that is worn by women in West African countries

Short Summary

Purple Hibiscus takes place in Enugu, a city in post-colonial Nigeria, and is narrated by the main character, Kambili Achike. Kambili lives with her older brother Jaja (Chukwuku Achike), a teenager who, like his sister, excels at school but is withdrawn and sullen. Kambili's father, Papa (Eugene Achike) is a strict authoritarian whose strict adherence to Catholicism overshadows his paternal love. He punishes his wife, Mama (Beatrice Achike), and his children when they fail to live up to his impossibly high standards.

The novel begins on Palm Sunday. Jaja has refused to go to church and receive communion. Because Jaja has no reasonable excuse for missing church, Papa throws his missal at his son. The book hits a shelf containing his wife's beloved figurines. This defiant act and resulting violence marks the beginning of the end of the Achike family. Kambili then explains the events leading up to Palm Sunday, detailing the seeds of rebellion that are planted in the children's minds by their liberal Aunty Ifeoma, Papa's sister.

Papa is a prominent figure in Enugu. He owns several factories and publishes the pro-democracy newspaper the Standard. He is praised by his priest, Father Benedict, and his editor, Ade Coker, for his many good works. Papa generously donates to his parish and his children's schools. His newspaper publishes articles critical of the rampant government corruption. Since the Standard tells the truth, the staff is under constant pressure from the Head of State, the military leader who assumes the presidency following a coup. When Ade Coker is arrested, Papa's bravery and position in the community help to free him.

Kambili is a quiet child. When she tries to speak, she often stutters or has a coughing fit. The rigid life that is shaped by her father renders her mute. Each day, she follows a schedule that allots only time to study, eat, sleep, pray and sit with her family. Kambili is a good student, rising to the top of her class. The girls at school assume she is a snob because she doesn't socialize and always runs straight to her father's car after class. When Kambili places second on term, Papa tells her she must excel because God expects more from her. Kambili is not a snob; she is motivated by fear, unable to create her own identity.

At Christmas, the family returns to the Papa's ancestral town, Abba. The family supervises a feast that feeds the entire umunna – extended family. Papa is celebrated for his generosity in Abba as well. However, he does not allow his children to visit with his own father, Papa-Nnukwu, for more than fifteen minutes each Christmas. Papa calls his father a "heathen" because he still follows the religious traditions of his people, the Igbo. When Aunty Ifeoma comes to visit from her University town of Nsukka, she argues with Papa about his mistreatment of their father. But Papa is firm. He will only acknowledge and support his father if he converts. Aunty Ifeoma invites Kambili and Jaja to visit so they can go on a pilgrimage to Aokpe, site of a miraculous apparition of the Virgin Mary. Papa begrudgingly agrees.

Nsukka is a different world. The University is beset by fuel shortages, pay stoppages, strikes at medical clinics, blackouts, and rising food prices. The widowed Aunty Ifeoma successfully raises her three children, Amaka, Obiora and Chima, with what little she has. But her family is a happy one. Unlike Papa, Aunty Ifeoma encourages her children to question authority, raising them with faith but also intellectual curiosity. Amaka and Kambili are very different girls. Amaka, like Kambili's classmates, assumes her cousin is a privileged snob since she does not know how to contribute to household chores. Kambili retreats into silence even in Nsukka. Jaja, on the other hand, blossoms. He follows the example of his younger cousin Obiora, concocting his own rite of initiation out of helping his family, tending a garden and killing a chicken. Kambili begins to open up when she meets Father Amadi. A Nigerian-born priest, Father Amadi is gentle and supportive. He encourages Kambili to speak her mind. Through Father Amadi, Kambili learns that it is possible to think for oneself and yet still be devout. She even begins speaking above a whisper to Amaka, and they become closer.

Kambili and Jaja learn to be more accepting in Nsukka. When he falls ill, Aunty Ifeoma brings Papa-Nnukwu to her flat. Kambili and Jaja decide not to tell Papa that they are sharing a home with a "heathen." Kambili witnesses her grandfather's morning ritual of innocence, where he offers thanks to his gods and proclaims his good deeds. She sees the beauty in this ritual and begins to understand that the difference between herself and Papa-Nnukwu is not so great. When her father finds out that Kambili and Jaja have spent time with their grandfather, he brings them home. Amaka gives her a painting of Papa-Nnukwu to take back to Enugu. Papa punishes his children by pouring hot water over their feet for "walking into sin."

Pressure mounts on Papa. Soldiers arrest Ade Coker again and torture him, and they raid the offices of the Standard and shut down his factories for health code violations. Shortly thereafter, the government murders Ade Coker. Tensions rise in the home too. Kambili and Jaja take comfort in the painting of Papa-Nnukwu. Papa catches them, however, and he beats Kambili so severely that she ends up in critical condition in the hospital. When she is well enough to be released, she goes to Nsukka instead of home. Her crush on Father Amadi intensifies and she begins to break out of her shell more, learning how to laugh and to join in the Igbo songs. But Aunty Ifeoma gets fired from the University and decides to go to America to teach. Kambili is floored. She is not sure what she will do without the refuge provided by her aunt and cousins. Amaka does not want to go to America either because her roots are in Nigeria.

Mama comes to Nsukka, limping out of a cab. Papa has beaten her again, causing another miscarriage. Though both Kambili and Jaja have seen this happen before, this time it is different. Aunty Ifeoma urges her not to return to Enugu. But she takes her children back with her. The following week is Palm Sunday, when Jaja refuses to go to church. In the week between Palm Sunday and Easter, Jaja grows increasingly defiant. He finally demands that he and Kambili spend Easter with their cousins. Weakened by what the children believe is stress, he allows them to go to Nsukka. A few days later, Mama calls. Papa has died. When Mama left Nsukka, she began poisoning her husband's tea. Jaja takes the blame for the crime and goes to prison.

The final chapter of the book takes place nearly three years later. Kambili and Mama visit a hardened Jaja in prison. He has faced severe punishments and miserable conditions over the course of his term. However, with the leadership in Nigeria now changing again, their lawyers are confident that Jaja will be released. Though Jaja has learned to not expect a favorable outcome, Kambili is overjoyed. She dreams that she will take Jaja to America to visit Aunty Ifeoma, together they will plant orange trees in Abba, and purple hibiscuses will bloom again.

Quotes and Analysis

Things started to fall apart when my brother, Jaja, did not go to communion and Papa flung his heavy missal across the room and broke the figurines on the étagère.

Kambili, Page 1

"Things fall apart" is an allusion to one of the most well-known English-language books about Nigeria. *Things Fall Apart,* by Chinua Achebe, chronicles the decline of an Igbo clan leader in the shadow of British colonial rule and Christian missionaries. *Purple Hibiscus* is a novel about a culturally Igbo family who lives under strict Catholic mores. Papa, the patriarch, was schooled in Britain and adopts and English-inflected accent when speaking in public. The Achike family reflects both the roots of their ancestry and the impact imperialism has had on their traditions.

I meant to say I am sorry that Papa broke your figurines, but the words that came out were, 'I'm sorry your figurines broke, Mama.'

Kambili, Page 10

As a victim of physical violence at the hands of father, Kambili is too frightened to speak the truth. Everything she wants to say she translates into what she should say. If Kambili were not the narrator of the novel, her true feelings would not be understood. The Achike family must always keep up appearances, hiding the truth about Papa. Even inside their home, Kambili cannot bring herself to blame Papa for the broken figures though the entire family witnessed his outburst. Kambili's misplaced sense of duty renders her mute.

'Imagine what the Standard would be if we were all quiet.'

It was a joke. Ade Coker was laughing; so was his wife, Yewande. But Papa did not laugh. Jaja and I turned and went back upstairs, silently.

Ade Coker; Kambili, Page 58

Though Papa and Ade Coker, through the Standard, seek to tell the truth about the government, the Achike children are not urged to tell the truth about their own lives. To Papa, being a good Nigerian entails two things – exposing corruption and strict adherence to faith. Papa believes it is his duty to deliver his country and his children to heaven. He holds both up to extreme standards. Though he is considered a hero for fighting against corruption, his actions as a disciplinarian in the home make him a monster. Ultimately, Papa is neither. He is a flawed person.

I looked at Jaja and wondered if the dimness in his eyes was shame. I suddenly wished, for him, that he had done the ima mmuo, the initiation into the spirit world. I knew very little about it; women were not supposed to know anything at all, since it was the first step toward the initiation to manhood. But Jaja once told me that he heard that boys were flogged and made to bathe in the presence of a taunting crowd. The only time Papa had talked about the ima mmuo was to say that the Christians who let their sons do it were confused, that they would end up in hellfire.

Kambili, Page 87

This is the beginning of Jaja's transformation. The Christmas holiday spent in the company of Aunty Ifeoma and, secretly, Papa-Nnukwu, is like an intiation ceremony of its own. Jaja is exposed to a different way of life both through the liberal beliefs of his aunt and the traditionalist rituals of his grandfather. Jaja compares himself to Obiora, who is well-spoken and mature for his age. Obiora has done the ima mmuo in his father's hometown. Though his father is dead, Obiora seems to have a deeper connection with his father's ancestors. Jaja is not permitted to visit with his grandfather for more than fifteen minutes a year. His shame at not taking part in the initiation prompts Jaja to question the authority of his father.

'I thought the Igwe was supposed to stay at his place and receive guests. I didn't know he visits people's homes,' Amaka said, as we went downstairs. 'I guess that's because your father is a Big Man.'

I wished she had said 'Uncle Eugene' instead of 'your father.' She did not even look at me as she spoke. I felt, looking at her, that I was helplessly watching precious flaxen sand slip away between my fingers.

Amaka; Kambili, Page 93

Amaka is not afraid to speak her mind. She does not offer Papa the same terse respect that Kambili is compelled to. Though Amaka is derisive towards her, Kambili longs to be understood by her cousin. Amaka represents an alternative version of herself – confident, inquisitive, and aware of her body. Kambili wants to be like her cousin even though she does not fully comprehend her ways.

When she made a U-turn and went back the way we had come, I let my mind drift, imagining God laying out the hills of Nsukka with his wide white hands, crescent-moon shadows underneath his nails just like Father Benedict's.

Kambili, Page 131

Quotes and Analysis

Kambili finds God in the natural world. The hands she envisions creating the hills of Nsukka are white, as she has been taught to accept a white image of God. Kambili's experiences with Aunty Ifeoma's family have opened her eyes to different types of faiths. Aunty Ifeoma herself successfully blends traditionalist ways with her Catholic faith. At this point, Kambili still clings to her ingrained understanding of faith.

'Morality, as well as the sense of taste, is relative.'

Obiora, Page 156

Obiora, as the son of a university professor of African studies, is encouraged to question authority. This statement opposes what Kambili and Jaja are taught. They are only offered one path towards success. This discourse is at the heart of the book. There are no moral absolutes in *Purple Hibiscus*. Kambili loves her father though he abuses her and her faith remains strong even when it is used as a tool for repression. Kambili learns this lesson on her journey.

'This cannot go on, nwunye m,' Aunty Ifeoma said. 'When a house is on fire, you run out before the roof collapses on your head.'

Aunty Ifeoma, Page 213

Aunty Ifeoma cannot believe that Mama would consider returning to her home after the beating-induced miscarriage. Aunty Ifeoma does not understand that the Achike family has been living in a burning house for a long time. In the early chapters of the novel, Mama suffers the same fate, losing a child because of Papa's violence. But this time, Mama listens to Aunty Ifeoma's plainspoken advice. Though she does return to Enugu, Mama begins poisoning Papa shortly thereafter.

Rain splashed across the floor of the veranda, even though the sun blazed and I had to narrow my eyes to look out the door of Aunty Ifeoma's living room. Mama used to tell Jaja and me that God was undecided about what to send, rain or sun. We would sit in our rooms and look out at the raindrops glinting with sunlight, waiting for God to decide.

Kambili, Page 217

Kambili's belief in God's connection to nature is inspired by Mama. Though she does not hold on to many traditional rituals outside of Igbo song, she draws parallels with the Catholic God and Chukwu. As God created the world and is omnipresent, Chukwu built the earth and is associated everything in it. Kambili is undecided as well. Her home is in Enugu, but having tasted a freer way of life in Nsukka, she feels conflicted about her future. She loves Papa but does not want to live in his shadow.

She picked up an enterprising snail that was crawling out of the open basket. She threw it back in and muttered, 'God take power from the devil.' I wondered if it was the same snail, crawling out, being thrown back in, and then crawling out again. Determined. I wanted to buy the whole basket and set that one snail free.

Kambili, Page 238

Kambili feels akin to the snail. She is trapped in the basket of her father's home and when she goes to Nsukka, she is crawling towards freedom. Though she may not recognize that she is as determined as the snail, her strength grows as it is nurtured by the love of her aunt and Father Amadi.

That night when I bathed, with a bucket half full of rainwater, I did not scrub my left hand, the hand that Father Amadi had held gently to slide the flower off my finger. I did not heat the water, either, because I was afraid that the heating coil would make the rainwater lose the scent of the sky. I sang as I bathed. There were more earthworms in the bathtub, and I left them alone, watching the water carry them and send them down the drain.

Kambili, Page 269-270

Kambili wants to bathe in the scent of the sky. The Igbo god Chukwu lives in the sky. Kambili wants to honor nature here and also retain the elements of her happy memories. She lets the earthworms be this time. Having found her voice, she sings. Here she revels in the natural world.

'Kambili is right,' she said. 'Something from God was happening there.'

Aunty Ifeoma, Page 275

Aunty Ifeoma notices that Father Amadi is looking at Kambili before she says this. Kambili is like a new girl. She is confident and happy, blossoming in the attention of her aunt's family and also Father Amadi. Her coming of age, complete with first crush, has been a gift from God. Even though she didn't see the apparition, Aunty Ifeoma saw new life in her niece.

'Of course God does. Look at what He did to his faithful servant Job, even to His own Son. But have you ever wondered why? Why did He have to murder his own son so we would be saved? Why didn't he just go ahead and save us?'

Jaja, Page 289

Quotes and Analysis

Jaja breaks with his faith at this point. His questioning of the Bible's parables has resonance in his own life. The treatment of the son by the father pertains to the abuse suffered at the hands of Papa as well. Papa, and his faith, is literally and figuratively dead to Jaja at this point.

'We will take Jaja to Nsukka first, and then we'll go to America to visit Aunty Ifeoma,' I said. 'We'll plant new orange trees in Abba when we come back, and Jaja will plant purple hibiscus, too, and I'll plant ixora so we can suck the juices of the flowers.' I am laughing. I reach out and place my arm around Mama's shoulder and she leans toward me and smiles.

Above, clouds like dyed cotton wool hang low, so low I feel I can reach out and squeeze the moisture from them. The new rains will come down soon.

Kambili, Page 306-307

Several themes are at play in this quote. Kambili's laughter signals that she has fully come in to her own, able to support herself as well as Mama. Her reverence for nature comes across in her planting of new orange trees in her ancestral town, a symbol of new life and new beginnings. Jaja's purple hibiscus, a symbol of freedom, will bloom again. The ixora plants were a favorite of Father Amadi, and the memories of when Kambili felt most whole will spring to life with a new planting of ixora. The "new rains" symbolize the hope of a new beginning, as the environment plays a major symbolic role in this novel. This book ends on a hopeful note.

Quotes and Analysis

Summary and Analysis of Chapter One

PART ONE – BREAKING GODS: PALM SUNDAY

Summary

Palm Sunday marks a change in the Achike household. Narrator Kambili, the 15-year old daughter of a devout Catholic, is terrified of the punishment her brother Jaja will incur for missing the day's mass. When the family arrives home from church, Papa demands an explanation from his son. Why did he not receive communion? Jaja says it is because the wafer gives him bad breath. Papa is shocked and reminds Jaja that not accepting the Host – the body of their Lord – is death. Jaja responds that he will die. Papa then throws his heavy leather-bound missal across the room, missing Jaja but breaking his wife's beloved figurines.

Kambili's Papa Eugene is a revered member of Enugu, Nigeria. A prominent and wealthy business leader, Eugene is praised by St. Agnes' white Father Benedict for using his power to spread the Gospel and speak the truth. However, inside his own home, he is a feared authoritarian and strict disciplinarian. Kambili notes the fading black eye of her Mama Beatrice. Kambili still takes pride in her father and his deeds, though he urges the family to stay humble.

Tensions rise in the Achike house throughout the day. Jaja helps his Mama clean up the jagged pieces of the figurines while Papa has his tea. Kambili is dismayed that her father does not offer her a "love sip" of his tea. Papa drinks quietly as if Jaja had not just talked back to him. Kambili goes up to her room and daydreams before lunch. She stares out over the expansive yard lined with frangipani, bougainvillea trees and hibiscus bushes. Mama's red hibiscuses are the pride of their parish. Each Sunday, flowers are plucked by Mama's prayer group members. Even the government officials who Jaja say try to bribe Papa cannot resist the hibiscus.

The usual Sunday routines do not occur. Mama does not plait Kambili's hair in the kitchen and Jaja does not go up to his own room to read before lunch. Kambili comes downstairs when lunch is served by Sisi, the servant girl. Papa says grace over the meal, a ritual lasting more than twenty minutes. He addresses the Blessed Virgin as Our Lady, Shield of the People of Nigeria, a title he has invented. The meal proceeds in silence until Mama mentions that a new product has been delivered to the house that afternoon – bottles of cashew juice from one of Papa's factories.

Papa pours a glass of the yellow liquid for each member of the family. Kambili hopes that if she praises the juice, Papa will forget that he has not yet punished Jaja for his insubordination. Both Kambili and Mama offer kind words to Papa about the juice. Jaja says nothing. Papa stares at his son and again demands an explanation. Jaja says he has no words in his mouth. He then excuses himself before Papa can give the final prayer. Kambili swallows all of her cashew juice and has a severe coughing fit.

Kambili spends the rest of the night sick in her room. Both Papa and Mama come to check on her, but she is nauseated and deep in thought about her brother. Mama offers her some soup, but Kambili vomits. She asks about Jaja, who did not visit her after dinner. Mama tells her daughter that Jaja did not come down for supper either. Kambili then asks about Mama's figurines. Mama will not replace them.

Kambili lies in bed and realizes that Papa's missal did not just break Mama's figurines. Everything was tumbling down. Kambili thinks Jaja's defiance is like the purple hibiscus in her Aunty Ifeoma's garden. They represent a new kind of freedom, unlike the chants of freedom shouted at the Government Center. The purple hibiscus represents a freedom to do and to be.

Analysis

Kambili narrates the book in the first person, but in the past tense. The book has a unique structure that begins with the events of Palm Sunday, as described in the first chapter. The next twelve chapters chronicle the events that culminate in Jaja skipping communion on Palm Sunday. The following four chapters detail the immediate aftermath of Palm Sunday. The final chapter, which is the indicated as the present, is three years after the events of the rest of the novel. Kambili, now eighteen years old, is narrating what happens to her and her family when she is fifteen. Through her eyes, we see the destruction of her family as well as the crumbling political situation of Nigeria. Told from a child's perspective, the novel is not overtly political and the debates on corruption unfold through conversation and overhearing. Since Kambili is not directly involved in activism, readers can draw their own conclusions about the political landscape from the personal experience of a young Nigerian. Her understanding of her family's pro-democracy stance is enhanced by her experiences with her liberal aunt.

Kambili's journey is a coming of age story set against multiple tyrannies. The corruption of her local government plays out in the background as Kambili is removed from direct strife due to her family's wealth. Her father's strict Catholic rule of their house is the greater tyranny Kambili must cope with. She alludes to emotions and events that will play out in the rest of the novel in the opening line, "Things started to fall apart at home when my brother, Jaja, did not go to communion..." We know there is trouble to come since the opening paragraph contains an eruption of violence. Though we do not see any abuse in this first chapter, Kambili's fear is palpable. Her concern for the well-being of her brother signifies not only the punishments they have received in the past, but also that Jaja's behavior is new. This is a coming of age story for Jaja as well.

Religion is at the forefront of the Achike family. Kambili's faith is strong as she has been raised to be a devout Catholic girl. However, religion in Nigeria and also for Kambili is more complicated than it appears. The white image of God was brought over by colonialist British missionaries. Conversion to Catholicism for many Nigerians means eradicating their roots and traditions. The Achikes do not participate in any "heathen" or "pagan" rituals and are therefore singled out as model Catholics. Kambili is led to believe that anything traditional is evil, so she is severed from her ancestry. Kambili grows aware of the hypocrisy of her father's position as religious leader. Though he is praised for his commitment to the truth as published in his newspaper, the Achikes are forbidden to tell the truth about the situation in their own home. Papa's punishments are attempts to make his children perfect in the eyes of both the community and God. He does not enjoy abusing his family, but he believes he must correct their behavior. Mama is less severe than Papa, often pointing out the more beautiful, natural world of God. Kambili takes solace in the natural world, especially in her mother's famous red hibiscuses. Mama's connection with nature and respect for the natural world represents another dimension of faith. Mama finds God in the natural world, not just in the rosary. Kambili's relationship with God is complex, consisting of the fear of hell instilled by Papa and the reverence for beauty instilled by Mama.

Their relationship with Papa is complex as well. Though it is clear that her father rules their household with an iron fist, a deep love for her Papa is evident. She swells with pride when Father Benedict praises Papa's deeds and charity. Kambili represents modern Africa, at a crossroads between colonial faith and traditional views. Her church does not allow any worship in Igbo, their native language. There is constant tension between the Igbo rituals and the rigid, Western mores of Catholicism. Jaja's heresy and insubordination is startling and Kambili becomes ill from the stress. Her coughing fit at dinner is a physical reaction to the change that has come over Jaja. As explored more fully in the next section, Kambili's repression manifests itself in a loss of words.

Jaja and Mama's actions are symbolic of the events that will unfold throughout the rest of the novel. When talking to her mother after supper, Kambili notes the recent scar on her face. Mama is a victim of Papa's abuse, but there is a sense that she will be putting a stop to the violence. As illustrated in the following section, Mama's figurines are a source of escapism from the tensions of home life. When she tells Kambili that she will not replace them, it is a signal that she is facing reality. Jaja's back-talk to his father signifies that he will no longer adhere to a faith he does not believe in simply because he is threatened by violence. Both Jaja and Mama are standing up to Papa.

Summary and Analysis of Chapter Two

PART TWO – SPEAKING WITH OUR SPIRITS: BEFORE PALM SUNDAY

Chapter Two

Summary

Mama brings Kambili's school uniform inside before it rains. Although it is not proper for older people to do chores, Mama does not mind. Kambili thinks there is a lot that Mama does not mind. Mama tells Kambili that she is pregnant, due in October. It is a relief for Mama. After Kambili was born, she suffered miscarriages. The women of their village gossiped about her, even suggesting Papa take other wives to help propagate the line. But Papa refused. Kambili agrees that her father should be praised – he is not like other men.

Mama hosts members of Our Lady of the Miraculous Medal, a prayer group consisting of women in Enugu. They pray and sing praise songs in Igbo, their native tongue. Mama prepares a lavish spread for the group, going above and beyond the normal fare. As she is the wife of one of the most prominent men in their village, she must uphold certain standards.

Jaja comes home from school, dressed in his crisp uniform. Last year he was named neatest boy at St. Nicholas, to the delight of Papa. Jaja goes to Kambili's room and they talk about Mama's baby. Kambili believes they speak a special language with their eyes – sharing thoughts that can't be spoken out loud. Jaja says the baby will be a boy, and they both promise to protect him. Though they do not say his name, they will protect him from Papa.

Jaja goes downstairs to eat lunch and Kambili glances at her schedule. Her father draws up a daily schedule for both of his children. Each activity is clearly delineated and must be strictly adhered to. Papa allows time for studying, prayer, family time, siesta, eating and sleeping. Kambili wonders when her father will create a schedule for her new brother.

The next day, during scheduled family time, the family plays chess and listens to the radio. A general comes on air and declares that a new coup has been carried out in Nigeria. The new head of state will be revealed the following day. Papa excuses himself to call Ade Coker, editor of the paper that Papa publishes. When he returns, Papa tells his family he is uneasy about the coup. In the 1960s, a cycle of bloody coups led to civil war. Military men will always violently overthrow other military men, he says.

Papa's paper, The Standard, is critical of its government. Ade Coker often runs scathing editorials, reporting on secret bank accounts of cabinet members who take money that belongs to the state. Even though the politicians are often corrupt, Papa wants a renewed democracy in his country. The Standard publishes an editorial the following day urging the new military head of state to implement a return to democratic rule.

Papa reads the headlines printed in other papers. He maintains the Standard is the only paper that tells the truth. His family praises his work, but he is not comforted. Papa thinks Nigeria is in decline. Kambili tells him God will deliver them. Papa nods and Kambili is pleased with the positive reinforcement.

Analysis

Mama brings Kambili her uniform even though it is not proper for older people to do the chores of young people. "…there was so much that Mama did not mind." Mama is thoughtful and caring and, in subtle ways, flouts convention if it is unreasonable. Unlike Papa, she will not insist on following only "what is done." It is a simple gesture, but meaningful in the context of the issues presented in the book – authority vs. reason, duty vs. love, and familial relationships. Though Mama is not as liberal and independent as Aunty Ifeoma, her love for her family allows her to break certain minor rules.

Mama's pregnancy is cause for much celebration as she has had miscarriages in the past. Her pregnancy will also quell town gossip. Papa has refused to take another mistress or wife even though propagating is traditionally the most important convention. Mama believes he should be praised for staying with her, as does Kambili. However, Papa is conforming to his Catholic beliefs. He does not consider enacting on any local, ancestral traditions. His strict adherence to his religion has both positive and negative effects on his family. Papa maintains the nuclear family unit, but lords his power over his children in the name of God. Religion is not deemed overall "good" or "bad." Faith is portrayed as realistically complex.

Religion can be corrupted by those who wield it. Aunty Ifeoma's children argue that Europeans introduced Christianity as a way to subdue the natives of countries they colonized. Papa's abuse of his family is his interpretation of wielding God's love. Power corrupts as well. Papa uses his prosperity for good, unlike government officials. He donates to charities and helps his neighbors in need. Papa is a man who lives by his own unique moral code. He is uncompromising in his fight for what he believes is right. News of the latest military coup makes Papa uneasy. Having witnessed several bloody coups culminating in a civil war, Papa understands that his country will face several difficulties in the future. Papa takes a stand against political corruption by publishing pro-democracy editorials in his newspaper. Papa cannot be considered either a hero or a villain, but rather a complicated human being.

It is important that the Achickes keep up appearances. Mama puts out a lavish spread for her prayer group, going above and beyond what is necessary. Papa takes pride in Jaja's award of neatest boy at school. The portrayal of the Achike family to the outside world must be spotless. Even though at home Papa allows himself a moment of pride in his work at the Standard, he insists his family be impassive when they are praised for the same deeds in church. The Achikes must be paragons of virtue, humble and faithful. But this moment of pride reveals hypocrisy in Papa. He holds his family to an impossible standard of perfection.

Kambili believes that she and her brother communicate through a secret language in their eyes. As illustrated by their respectful silence both in church and at home, speaking the truth is not an option. Jaja tells Kambili that they will protect their new brother, but do not dare to utter that it is from Papa that he will be protected. Though Kambili, 15, and Jaja, 17, are teenagers, they are sheltered and immature for their age. The considerable strain placed on their backs by their father has rendered them childlike. Kambili's secret language reveals an innocence but also a naivete. This is the beginning of a coming-of-age story.

Summary and Analysis of Chapter Three

Summary

In the weeks following the coup, Kambili notices a change in the atmosphere. As articles in the Standard are growing more critical and questioning, the other papers read at family time seem more subdued than usual. When Kevin, the driver, takes the kids to school, they pass demonstrators at the Government Center. The car bears green branches, a symbol of solidarity with the activists, so that they may pass through the fray. Kambili wonders what it would be like to join their cause, but she can only watch from the car window. In later weeks, Kambili notes an escalation of military presence. Soldiers line the main road armed with guns. They search cars at will, holding the drivers at the side of the road at gunpoint.

But nothing changes at home except for Mama's growing belly. The family goes to mass on Pentecost Sunday. Mama wears a red wrapper the same color as the visiting priest's robe. The priest gives his sermon but does not openly praise St. Agnes as other visiting priests have in the past. He also sings a song in Igbo and the congregation is shocked. Many sing along, but Papa eyes his family to make sure their lips are sealed.

On the way to visit Father Benedict after mass, Papa derides the visiting priest. He claims he is godless and people like him who blend traditional African ways with the church are troublemakers. When they arrive, Mama decides to stay in the car because she feels ill. Papa stares at her, then asks again if she will come in to see Father Benedict. She insists that she doesn't feel right but after a stern silence, she finally agrees to get out of the car.

Papa talks to Father Benedict in hushed tones while the rest of the family waits in the living room. Father Benedict asks Mama if she is okay because she looks so ashen. She says her allergies are bothering her but she is fine. Father Benedict then asks Kambili and Jaja if they enjoyed the sermon. As if rehearsed, they both answer the same way at the same time, with a simple "Yes, Father." After the visit, Mama insists on serving Papa his tea even though this duty usually falls to Sisi.

Papa gives Jaja and Kambili "love sips" of the tea and then the children go to their rooms to change out of their church clothes. They follow Mama up the stairs in silence. All Sunday activities are quiet – the children are scheduled reflection time to study a particular passage in the Bible in addition to evening rosary. Jaja tells Mama that she should rest and before she can answer, she covers her mouth and runs to her room to vomit.

Lunch is silent as well. Kambili waits for the prayer, thinking about the birds outside and looking at a portrait of her Grandfather. Her father finally speaks, offering first thanks for the food. He then asks God to forgive those who wish to thwart His will by not wanting to visit His servant. Mama's "Amen" resonates throughout the room.

After lunch, Kambili is in her room studying the Bible when she hears loud thuds coming from her parents' room. This is a familiar sound. She sits and closes her eyes while counting. Usually the noises end by the time she reaches twenty. By nineteen, her father leaves his room with Mama slung over his shoulder. Jaja and Kambili watch as he takes her outside. Jaja notices there is blood on the floor. They scrub the floor clean.

Mama does not come home that evening and Kambili and Jaja eat dinner alone. They talk about a televised execution of three men. Jaja says grace, offering a small prayer for Mama. Papa comes home later, his eyes red and swollen. He hugs Kambili and tells her Mama will be fine - back tomorrow after school. Mama does come home the next day and informs her daughter that the baby is gone. Mama consoles herself by polishing her beloved ballerina figurines.

Kambili goes upstairs to study, but the words in her textbook turn to blood. She envisions blood flowing from Mama and from her own eyes. At Mass on Sunday, Papa makes his family stay in church after the service so that they can recite sixteen novenas for Mama's forgiveness. Father Benedict douses them in holy water and Kambili tries not to think about what Mama would need to be forgiven for.

Analysis

Tensions are rising both in Nigeria and in the Achike household. The political unrest is increasing, with pro-democracy activists assembling near Government Centers. The increased presence of soldiers and dangerous road blocks create an environment rife with violence. Even the televised executions don't elicit much reaction from Kambili and Jaja. They are already living in the shadow of violence. They are so desensitized to violence that they wordlessly clean up their mother's blood after she suffers a severe beating.

Kambili watches the protestors from the safety of her car, wondering what it would be like to join them. Her wealth protects her from the more dangerous aspects of life, but it also shelters her. However, this is a false sense of security. From inside the same car, Papa demands Mama overcomes her sickness to visit with Father Benedict. From the outside, the Achikes have a perfect existence but Kambili's life is far from ideal.

Mama continues to keep up appearances by insisting to Father Benedict her allergies are the cause of her ashen look. She must maintain the illusion that she is strong and happy. Although she sings Igbo songs with her prayer group, she does not dare sing along with the visiting priest during the day's mass. Papa eyes his family to make sure they stay silent. Even though Mama's nod to her ancestral culture is permitted at home, the Achikes must maintain a colonial attitude in public. Again, the image of perfection must be upheld.

Both Mama and Kambili find outlets for escapism. Throughout a tense, silent lunch, Kambili concentrates on the picture of her maternal Grandfather and the chirping of birds in the garden. The portrait of her Grandfather in full Catholic missionary garb serves as inspiration at first. Kambili strives to hold the same position of honor as her Grandfather, who was beloved by Papa. She wants to be beloved by Papa and believes by emulating her Grandfather's godliness, she will earn his respect. Mama polishes her figurines as a distraction from the palpable disappointment of her husband. When they break in the first chapter, the illusions come crashing down.

The reality that must not be spoken is the abuse. When Kambili hears repetitive thuds from her parents' room, she knows what is happening. Even though the incident is told through first-person narration – ostensibly, Kambili's thoughts – the abuse is not directly stated. Kambiil's childlike naivete betrays itself here. As a child in need of protection, her own mind guards her from the truth. To not speak the truth is to deny its existence. Furthermore, pain and love are interwoven in her mind. When she takes a "love sip" of Papa's tea she "feels the love burning on her tongue." The discipline is synonymous with love.

There is a patriarchal hierarchy in the Achike household. Mama and the children do not have any power. When Mama loses her child as the result of a severe beating, Papa makes the family say a special prayer, a novena, to atone for the loss. Papa explains that they must ask for Mama's forgiveness. Sexism is inherent in both traditional and colonial African society. Even liberated Aunty Ifeoma is told by her father in Chapter Six that she "doesn't count" because she is a girl. But where Ifeoma, with her wisdom, intelligence and fortitude, can brush away such insults, Mama takes them to heart. Mama, raised by an austere Catholic, marries an austere Catholic and is privy to no other way of life. Mama abides the sexism and Kambili, in the end of this chapter, does not even want to think about why she needs to be forgiven. But that is about to change.

Summary and Analysis of Chapter Four

Summary

Ade Coker's wife Yewande comes to the Achike house in tears. Jaja sneaks down to the kitchen and listens. He tells Kambili that Ade has been arrested by soldiers on his way home from the Standard. His car has been abandoned, the driver's door left open. Kambili thinks he was arrested because of his article accusing the Head of State and his wife of paying people to transport heroin abroad. Papa assures Yewande that her husband will be protected by God.

At school, Kambili receives her report card. Although Mother Lucy, the principal at Daughters of the Immaculate Heart, praises her intelligence and obedience, Kambili is disappointed that she is ranked only second. Papa will not be proud. He often tells his children he does not spend so much money on tuition so that his children can be second. His godless father never paid a cent for his own education and he always ranked first.

Mama is waiting by the door to greet them with a song in Igbo. Kambili tells her she ranked only second and Mama pauses. She knows too well that Papa will not be pleased. Papa comes home and visits Jaja's room first. Jaja is ranked first, as always, and Papa takes his time. When he gets to Kambili's room, she is terrified. He does not punish her now, only asks her who came in first.

At dinner, the family samples a new biscuit produced at Papa's factory. The family praises his work. Afterwards, Papa tells Kambili to come upstairs. She follows him to his room and she sits on the bed and takes off her slippers, sinking her toes into the plush cream carpet. His room looks like heaven – Kambili fondly remembers the times Papa would comfort her here when she was a child. He tells her that she did not come in first because she chose not to. Kambili braces herself, but a phone call interrupts them. Papa is preoccupied by Ade Coker's ordeal.

Kambili waits to be punished. Even when Ade Coker is released from jail a week later, her report card is not mentioned. Ade thanks Papa in the Standard and Kambili takes pride in her father's bravery. Though Ade does not publicly talk about his time in prison, Papa learns he was tortured. Cigarettes were put out on his back. Papa decides that they will publish the Standard underground to keep the staff safe.

Mama takes Jaja and Kambili to the market to buy new sandals and bags before the new school term. The market is a different world from their estate – women loudly haggle with vegetable sellers, men freely urinate against walls, merchants fight over customers. This time, the market is even more chaotic than usual as soldiers hassle the village women and demolish vegetable stands. Mama ushers her children into the car, but watches a woman crying desperately in the dirt.

Papa drives Kambili to school on her first day back. Daughters of the Immaculate Heart is protected by high walls erected to keep hawkers out. At his request, Kambili takes her father to her classroom. They are intercepted by Sister Margaret who thanks him for his generous donation to renovate the library. As he speaks to her, Papa changes his accent so that he sounds more British.

Papa asks Kambili to point out Chinwe Yideze, the girl who came in first. He asks her how many heads she has. Then he takes out a mirror and asks how many heads Kambili has. Papa tells her that since she has one head, just as Chinwe has, there is no excuse to come second. Chinwe is not special. Papa tells her that since they are privileged, God expects more out of her. He leaves her to join her classmates at assembly.

The new term is begins with assembly. The students sing a welcoming song from the Catholic Hymnal and Mother Lucy reads from the Bible. The national anthem and pledge follow, a new ritual at Kambili's school. Only the Nigerian Sisters sing the anthem. Mother Lucy chooses Kambili to lead the pledge and she panics. She finally stutters the opening lines and the rest of the class joins in.

Kambili's friend Ezinne greets her and asks if she traveled over break. Kambili yearns to thank Ezinne for talking to her and not calling her a "backyard snob" as the rest of the girls do. Chinwe, clearly the most popular girl in school, says hello to Ezinne and other classmates. She has never talked to Kambili so she passes right by her. Ezinne gossips, telling Kambili that Chinwe buys Coke and biscuits for the other students at break. They flock to her because she is rich and outgoing. Chinwe started calling Kambili "backyard snob" because she is so quiet, choosing to spend breaks in the library instead of with others. Chinwe assumes Kambili feels too big to socialize. Kambili cannot tell Ezinne the truth – she runs home because she is not allowed to be late. Everything she does is to prevent punishment.

Analysis

Papa takes his family's privilege very seriously. In a country that is wracked with poverty, the Achike wealth must be justified by duty. He tells Kambili, "Because God has given you much, he expects much from you." There is no excuse for coming in second place. His father did not pay for his own education, yet he always strove to be the best. Papa demands excellence from his children and gets results only by instilling fear in them. After he leaves, Kambili joins her classmates in the assembly. When Mother Lucy calls on her to lead the pledge, Kambili chokes up. By invoking God in his speech, Papa equates failure with sin. She is terrified to make one false step, and therefore cannot even handle a simple task.

However, Kambili does have fond memories of her father. When she is called into his room to, presumably, be punished, she slips off her shoes and digs her toes into the plush white carpet. This room carries memories of both punishment and protection. While waiting for a potential beating, Kambili remembers being enveloped by a cream-colored blanket during a storm. This moment of fatherly love is a memory she holds on to. It is a symbol of paternal love that has been fractured by the severe punishments. Since Kambili, at this point, cannot imagine another way of life, she chooses to cling to the good memories to distract her from the pain.

There is a storm in Nigeria. Before Kambili can be punished, Papa is called away with news of Ade Coker's arrest. Papa is a man that is balancing his filial duty with his duty as a citizen. He applies a sliding scale of morality to the men who work for him at the Standard. Papa gives them bonuses and vacation as a way to protect them from the government's wrath. Papa is aghast when he learns about Ade's torture. However, he inflicts physical torment on his own family. Papa can rationalize these two paradoxical beliefs because he is doing God's work. He is saving his family from damnation and speaking out against corruption.

At the market, the presence of the soldiers is disquieting. Mama and the children watch a woman harassed by these men while shopping. Unlike with the rioters, they are near to the violence. Mama ushers her children into the car quickly, but the emotional effect of seeing the hassled woman in the dirt has already taken its toll. Mama does not tell her children to look away, as she did at the roadblock. Here, she watches the woman scream in despair as the car pulls away. She sympathizes with the woman even though she is protected by her status. This is the first instance where Mama identifies with a victim, recognizing herself in the face of someone less fortunate.

Kambili is perceived by her classmates as a backyard snob. For most of the novel, Kambili is unable to defend herself from such casual slander because she is saddled with having to both avoid punishment and distract from the truth. When her father visits her school, he speaks in the same British-inflected English he uses with Father Benedict. Just as Papa disguises his voice to portray a more polished persona, Kambili disguises her personal misfortune. Her wealth is a sticking point with the classmates who dislike her. Class tensions hamper the relationship with her cousin as well. Because she is unable to tell anyone of her responsibilities, in their eyes she behaves oddly. Though Kambili is called a snob, she is the exact opposite. Her self-worth is tied to her father's judgment.

Summary and Analysis of Chapter Five

Summary

By the end of the term, Kambili remains the backyard snob, carrying the heavy burden of besting Chinwe in her studies. At December break, she receives a report card with 1/25 written at the top. She is ranked first. The family prepares to spend Christmas in Abba Town, where Papa was raised. The cars are loaded with supplies - beans, rice, yams, plantains and liquor. They drive out of their gated street towards the commercial section Ninth Mile, reciting 10 rosaries apiece. Papa buys only bread and okpa (beans), but he gives money to all of the many hawkers who descend upon their car.

As they drive to their sprawling estate in Abba Town, villagers wave to Papa and call him "Omelora." In Abba, he has earned an honorary title that means "One Who Does For The Community." Boys run with the car into their compound and Papa gives them each a 10 Naira note. As Omelora, Papa and the Achike family provide for the town. Sisi unloads the cooking equipment that will be used to prepare enough food for the entire village. Mama and Sisi do not cook, but will supervise the women of the umunna (extended family) in the Achike compound. This is Christmas tradition followed by all prominent members of Abba Town.

Ade Coker, his wife and children stop by on their way to Lagos. Ade is playful with his children, throwing his infant up in the air. He tries to laugh with Kambili and Jaja, but they only respond to his questions with a yes or no. Ade tells Papa that his kids are always so quiet. Papa agrees – his children are not like noisy, undisciplined kids with no fear of God. Ade wonders what the Standard would be like if everyone at the paper was quiet, too.

In Abba, Jaja and Kambili do not have schedules. Papa is kept busy with town business, church meetings and his duties as chief of the umunna. He agreed to take the title only when all pagan undertones were removed from the ceremony. His title-taking ceremony filled the home's four floors. These days, the family occupies only the first two. Kambili feels the emptiness. Their morning prayers are interrupted by visitors, but Papa implores them to wait in the living room. After reciting their usual prayers, Papa concludes with a twenty minute prayer for the people of Nigeria. He includes a wish for his own father's conversion.

Papa-Nnukwu, Papa's father, follows the traditions of the Igbo people. Papa thinks he is a heathen and has offered him luxuries in exchange for converting to Christianity. Papa-Nnukwu refuses. Each Christmas, however, Jaja and Kambili are allowed to spend 15 minutes at Papa-Nnukwu's home. Papa sends a slim wad of cash to his father as well, but does not visit himself. Papa-Nnukwu is not permitted in their home either.

Jaja and Kambili go to Papa-Nnukwu's meager home. They exchange pleasantries, Papa-Nnukwu complimenting both children on their growth. He offers them food, but they refuse since they have been ordered to do so by their father. Since Papa-Nnukwu offers his food to his ancestors in a ritual each morning, Papa will not allow his Christian children to eat with their grandfather. Kambili cannot believe her father and his sister, Aunty Ifeoma, grew up in this tiny place. After their allotted time, Jaja nudges Kambili to get up. But she wants to stay, to watch over her grandfather. Finally, she rises, and they say goodbye.

Papa accuses Jaja and Kambili of staying longer than fifteen minutes with their grandfather. He does not hit them, as Kambili expects him to do, but he orders them to pray for forgiveness. Papa then throws out a heathen member of his umunna who is about Papa-Nnukwu's age. Papa does not respect his elders unless they share his faith. Kambili remembers the way Papa treated Mama's father. A light-skinned missionary, Grandfather was revered by Papa. Kambili remembers that he used the word sinner in nearly every sentence. His portrait hangs in Enugu in a place of pride.

Analysis

Ade Coker compliments Papa on the good behavior of his children but is also amused by their silence. He says, "Imagine what the Standard would be if we were all quiet." Papa does not laugh at Ade's joke. He is proud that he has raised his children with a fear in God. Ade and his writers do not fear the government even though they pose a risk to their careers and lives. For Papa, the government does not have authority because he disagrees with them. Again, this is evidence of Papa's sliding scale of morality.

In his ancestral home, Papa is considered one of the patriarchs of the umunna, or extended family. He has done his best to remove traditionalist rituals from all celebrations in his home. The people of Abba rejoice when he comes to town because his family is tasked with hosting the entire umunna on Christmas. Papa's charity is not limited to just this feast; Papa gives 10 naira notes to the local children and donates to the church. However, his charity makes him uncomfortable because the town does not abide by the strict measures Papa demands. The church garishly announces the amount he donates and the villagers have not abandoned its traditionalist ways. But since God expects him to give back, he has no choice but continue doling out money. His home is lavishly appointed, but his children do not enjoy any of the fineries. Papa puts on a show of his wealth because he is expected to. He does not authentically enjoy his works.

Heathens are not allowed in Papa's home. His own father, Papa-Nnukwu has never step foot in his sprawling mansion. Mama's father, known simply as Grandfather, is revered because he was a Catholic missionary. Kambili does not talk about her Grandfather often, other than to note he used the word "sinner" in almost every sentence. It is clear there is no bond between Kambili and her Grandfather. He is a looming figure synonymous with his faith, devoid of personality. When Kambili and

Jaja visit Papa-Nnukwu for their allotted fifteen minutes, Kambili searches for godlessness in his face. She doesn't find anything. Moreover, she wishes to stay and take care of her grandfather. There is a connection to her ancestors that her father is not able to blot out.

When a man his father's age comes to share in the feast, Papa throws him out. He echoes a sentiment that Papa-Nnukwu states in the following chapter. Papa's faith equates Jesus, the son, with God, the father. Papa can boss around his elders because he believes he is their equal. His faith erodes his traditional sense of familial duty and imbues him with a power over those who do not believe. His own son, even at 17, is not allowed an equal standing as his father.

The relationship between faith and money is complicated. As evidenced by the exchanges with both the priest in Abba and with Mother Lucy, charity manifests itself monetarily. Papa has offered his father luxuries he cannot afford if he is willing to convert. Papa-Nnukwu refuses to trade his faith for money. There is corruption evident in the church and corruption in Papa's power.

Summary and Analysis of Chapter Six

Summary

Papa's widowed sister Aunty Ifeoma arrives the next day with her children. She is the opposite of her brother – lively, playful and quick to laugh. Aunty Ifeoma calls Mama nwunye m, Igbo for "my wife." Although she is a Christian, she retains some of her traditional upbringing. Mama explains to Kambili that it means she is accepted. Mama and Ifeoma talk about the gossip in their respective umunnas. Ifeoma's in-laws spread rumors that she killed her beloved husband. Mama's umunna often urges her husband to take another wife. Mama was grateful to have Ifeoma on her side. She says she doesn't know what she would have done if Papa left her. Aunty Ifeoma says sometimes life begins after marriage.

Kambili watches and listens to her aunt intently, almost hypnotized by her manner and bronze lipstick. Aunty Ifeoma complains that life at the University in Nsukka, where she teaches, is getting increasingly difficult. Teachers have not been paid in two months and some have emigrated to America. Aunty Ifeoma can no longer afford cooking gas. Mama urges her to ask her brother for help. She insists the situation is not that dire. Papa emerges and he begrudgingly obliges Aunty Ifeoma's request to take Kambili and Jaja the following day for "sightseeing." She does not tell him that part of the trip will entail seeing the Aro festival, a traditional Igbo parade of masquerading spirits called mmuo.

Kambili's cousins arrive: Amaka, 15, an inquisitive teenage girl, Obiora, 14, an intelligent and assured boy, and Chima, big for his seven years. All kids share their mother's throaty laugh. Amaka asks if they can watch CNN on the Achike's satellite TV. Kambili nearly chokes every time Amaka speaks to her, but she manages to explain they don't watch much TV. Amaka sneers and asks if she is bored with satellite. Kambili lets the insult pass and does not tell her cousin the truth – TV time is not in her schedule. When they leave, Obiora and Chima say goodbye. Amaka does not turn back to her cousin.

The next day, Aunty Ifeoma picks up Kambili and Jaja. She suggests to Kambili that she change into trousers, but she politely declines. Kambili again does not tell her aunt the truth – she owns no trousers because it is sinful for women to wear pants. Kambili and Jaja pile into the car, Mama watching as they drive away. Aunty Ifeoma announces they will pick up Papa-Nnukwu first and Kambili's stomach lurches. Jaja and Kambili do not get out of the car at Papa-Nnukwu's home. Kambili explains that, though they were allowed to visit him briefly, they must keep their distance from pagans. Aunty Ifeoma shakes her head. Papa-Nnukwu climbs into the car and he jokes about dying soon. There is a familiarity to their banter. Kambili and Jaja do not laugh at any of their jokes.

Aunty Ifeoma's car passes Papa's house and Papa-Nnukwu sighs. Though his son owns a huge compound, there is often nothing on his plate. He blames the missionaries for leading Papa astray. Aunty Ifeoma interjects that she went to a missionary school as well, and she still takes care of her father. Papa-Nnukwu teases her, but continues his story about the first missionary in Abba. A white priest, Father John, gathers the local children and teaches them his religion. Papa-Nnukwu asked the priest about his God. Father John replies that his God is not unlike Chukwu, Papa-Nnuwku's god, because he lives in the sky. Papa-Nnukwu also asked him about the man on the cross. Father John told him he is Jesus, God's son, and they are equal. Papa-Nnukwu cannot believe that father and son would be equal. He thinks his own son disrespects him because he believes he is equal.

The car arrives at the Aro festival. Aunty Ifeoma points out the parading mmuo, which Papa had once deemed devilish folklore. But they do not look dangerous to Kambili. A person dressed as a woman spirit with a carved wooden mask and rouged lips stops to dance. Crowds cheer and throw naira at her while boys play music. Papa-Nnukwu instructs the women to look away from a mmuo with a grimacing human skull mask. A tortoise is tied to his head and a snake and three dead chickens hang from his costume. Women run fearfully. Papa-Nnukwu explains that he is the most powerful. Jaja asks how the people get into the costumes and Papa-Nnukwu hushes him, insisting they are spirits. He asks Jaja if he had done his imo mmuo, the initiation into the spirit world which is the first step towards manhood. Jaja says no, shame in his eyes.

Aunty Ifeoma drops off a sleepy Papa-Nnukwu and then Kambili and Jaja. She asks her children if they would like to go inside and Amaka answers no in such a way that makes her brothers also decline. Aunty Ifeoma waves to Papa, then hugs Kambili and Jaja tightly. That night, Kambili dreams she is laughing, but the voice is not her own. Her aunty's throaty, enthusiastic laugh escapes her own lips.

Analysis

Aunty Ifeoma and Mama are two very different women. Though Aunty Ifeoma grew up with Papa, she is a liberated woman who speaks her mind. Mama dismisses Ifeoma's arguments as "university talk." Mama has no use for logic that does not apply to her situation. Mama buys into the patriarchal paradigm. Papa is the head of the household and she is proud of his accomplishments and how they reflect on her family. Papa offers the same luxuries to Aunty Ifeoma and her children, but she refuses to submit to his will. Despite their different perspectives, Aunty Ifeoma and Mama love each other. Using a phrase common to the umunna, Aunty Ifeoma refers to Mama as "my wife," and the women support one another. Kambili notes that her mother speaks more with Aunty Ifeoma. Both are struggling with their own hardships, but love bonds them together.

Like their mothers, Kambili and Amaka are very different. Though both girls are 15, Amaka is self-assured. She wears lipstick like her mother, laughs like her mother, and does not openly praise Papa just because she is supposed to. From the outset,

Amaka has a disdain for Kambili. Like her classmates, Amaka assumes her reticence is a product of her economic class. When Kambili is unable to answer why her family does not watch much satellite TV, Amaka assumes she is bored by her luxuries. Amaka is being raised by a single parent. The privileges that Kambili can afford seem wondrous, but they leave her feeling bitter about her own station in life. Though she is liberal like her mother, Amaka is close-minded when it comes to class. Kambili, unable to speak for herself, allows Amaka to believe her life is rosy. But nothing is as simple as it appears. Amaka and her brothers are poor but loved and encouraged and Kambili is wealthy yet troubled.

When Aunty Ifeoma picks up Papa-Nnukwu, Kambili and Jaja do not get out of the car. This is reminiscent of the tense scene inside the Achike family car outside of Father Benedict's house. Aunty Ifeoma is lighter, more amused than angry, at the children's unwillingness to leave the safety of the car. She is gently trying to urge reason into their minds. Although Papa asks Mama if she would like to get of the car, his question carries the threat of violence. His question is a command and not a conversation. Kambili and Jaja do not get out of the car at Papa-Nnukwu's, but they also do not refuse to spend the day with him. Kambili wonders if they will get caught and, if so, what the punishments will be from both Papa and God.

The Aro Festival is unlike any ritual the Achike children have witnessed. A parade of men and women dressed in spirit costumes, this taste of ancestral ritual is both forbidden and tantalizing. Unfamiliar with its meaning, Jaja makes the mistake of asking how the people get inside the costumes. Papa-Nnukwu tells him that they are not people, but mmuo now. The ritual makes the people spirits. Jaja is ashamed that he does not know anything about his culture.

Jaja is also ashamed that he has not done the initiation, the first step towards manhood. Obiora, two years his junior, has done so. At seventeen, Jaja is not yet a man but he should have been taking steps toward adulthood. Papa and his religion preclude him from growing up. From this point on, Jaja begins his own initiation ritual by subtly challenging the authority of his father until Palm Sunday.

Kambili's dreams are an important motif. In her dreams, she allows herself to process what she cannot say. Here, she dreams that she laughs Aunty Ifeoma's laugh. In real life, she barely speaks above a whisper let alone laugh. She wishes she can speak the words Aunty Ifeoma speaks. She wishes she can be free.

Summary and Analysis of Chapter Seven

Summary

On their way into mass on Christmas Day, Kambili and her family pass Aunty Ifeoma and her children. Kambili fixates on the red lipstick worn by both her aunt and Amaka. Her mind strays to it during the sermon, spoken entirely in Igbo unlike at her usual church. The priest talks about money and corruption rather than the usual Christmas iconography, to the unease of Papa. The Achikes sit in the first pew, a place of honor, next to the only two men more prominent than Papa – Chief Umedi and the Igwe of Abba. After mass, they go to a fundraiser for the church. Papa writes out a large check quietly and is aghast when the MC broadcasts the amount. The priest dances garishly and Papa ushers his family outside.

They find their home crowded with people. The entire clan has come to eat in their compound. The women of the umunna coo over Jaja, next in line for Papa's money. Aunty Ifeoma and her children arrive for lunch. Kambili's cousins are enamored with the luxuries of the Achike home – the stereo, fine plates, creams in the bathroom. The Igwe arrives and Aunty Ifeoma and Amaka bow out of respect. Though the Igwe converted, he still carries out pagan traditions, so Papa allows his family to shake his hand rather than bow.

Kambili overhears her mother telling Aunty Ifeoma to ask her brother for the factory's spare gas cylinders. Aunty Ifeoma has refused his help in the past because Papa expected her to join the missionary Knights of St. John, to send Amaka to convent school, and even to stop wearing makeup. Ifeoma reminds Mama of her deceased husband's disagreements with Papa. Papa does not like confrontation or honesty. Ifeoma continues, saying her father will die soon and yet Papa refuses to see him. She says God is big enough to do his job, he does not need Papa to judge for him.

Over lunch, Aunty Ifeoma invites Kambili and Jaja to Nsukka for a visit. Papa insists that the children do not like to be away from home, but he will think about it. After a tense moment between the Papa and Ifeoma, a new bottle of juice is brought to the table. Amaka asks Papa if it is from his factory, then criticizes the sugar content. Kamblii's throat closes when she hears her cousin's retort. She knocks over her glass of juice, staining the table red. She is reminded of her mother's blood. Ifeoma tells Papa that she is planning a pilgrimage to a holy apparition in Aokpe. Though the miracle has not been verified by the church, he agrees to send Kambili and Jaja to Ifeoma's to join the pilgrimage. Kambili and Jaja will spend a week with their cousins in Nsukka.

Kambili wakes with her period the next morning. Mama decides to give her medication for her painful cramps. The Achike family fasts every Sunday before mass, not eating until they return home from Church. However, Kambili's medication can't be taken on an empty stomach. Mama gives her a bowl of cornflakes to eat quickly before Papa comes upstairs. But he catches her. Jaja tries to convince his father that he is responsible. He removes his belt and lashes at his entire family, asking them why they walk into sin. When he stops, a weight falls on him. He hugs his children and asks if they are hurt. Kambili says no, but they all change their clothes and wash their faces before Mass.

After New Year's, the Achikes leave Abba. Their umunna kneels in the dirt to thank the family, taking the leftover food home with them. One man tells Kambili that Papa pays his children's school fees. Papa is a great man, he tells her. On the way home, they see an accident near a government-erected roadblock. Though Mama tells the children to look away, Kambili thinks about the dead man on the rest of the trip. She wonders where he is going.

Two days later is the feast of the Epiphany, a Christian holiday celebrating the revelation that Jesus was the son of God. After mass, Papa takes his family to Father Benedict's house. Father Benedict hears the confessions of the Achike family. Papa first, rambling like a motor, then Mama, softly spoken, then Jaja, who takes the least amount of time, then Kambili. After confessing her sins, Father Benedict asks her if she is hiding something. She realizes Papa must have mentioned something to Father Benedict, but she can't think of what it could be. Father Benedict prompts her, asking about pagan rituals. She confesses her longer visit with Papa-Nnukwu and enjoying the mmuo masquerade.

The family drives home. Papa is overjoyed, telling them if they died right then, they would ascend to heaven. At home, he tells Kambili and Jaja that they are allowed to go to Aokpe as long as they realize the miracle has not yet been confirmed by the church. They will spend five days in Nsukka with Aunty Ifeoma. Mama suggests they offer a gas cylinder as a gift, asking Papa for the favor Ifeoma won't. The children pack, sharing joy with their eyes. They leave the following day. Papa thrusts their schedules for the week into Kambili and Jaja's hands.

Analysis

Everyone in Abba says that Papa is a good man. They detail his good works to Kambili and Jaja who say nothing in response. The pressure of keeping up appearances renders them silent. How could they respond? Papa is the benevolent father of his umunna, but he is not benevolent with his own children. His love extends to his umunna by way of money. But Kambili and Jaja know the true price of Papa's love: perfection at all costs.

Kambili focuses on Amaka's red lipstick throughout church. As Jaja compares himself to Obiora intellectually, Kambili compares herself to Amaka physically. She notes her tight clothing, her modern hair, and her makeup. Amaka is a mystery to Kambili because womanhood is a mystery. Papa does not allow Kambili to wear pants, let alone makeup, so Kambili grasps clues of her own budding sexuality where she can. In Nsukka, her crush on Father Amadi is an awakening but her cousin's dress and demeanor are the more important signifiers of adulthood.

Kambili is punished for breaking fast before mass. Experiencing painful cramps because of her period, she tries to take medicine. Ironically, the medication causes more pain in the form of a beating. To Papa, there are no mitigating circumstances that warrant flexibility. Kambili is beaten, but so are Jaja and Mama for letting Kambili sin. Her period, like initiation, is the first step towards adulthood. Her blood echoes the red juice that is spilled on the table. Kambili is reminded of her mother's blood.

After confession, Papa tells his children that they would all ascend to heaven if they died at that moment. He is smiling and drumming on the steering wheel. Later, in chapter ten, Kambili sees Papa-Nnukwu smile deeply after his own morning ritual. She notes that she and Jaja never smile when they say the rosary. The rejoicing that both Papa and Papa-Nnukwu experience is untouchable by Kambili and Jaja since it carries the burden of punishment. They are only allowed to revel in the thought of an afterlife.

Knowing of Aunty Ifeoma's financial troubles, Mama negotiates with Papa for a few spare gas cylinders to be taken from his factory to Nsukka. Papa assumes Aunty Ifeoma has asked for the hand-out, but Mama ensures him that she is working alone. By adopting a submissive position, Mama is able to get what she wants. She knows that Papa will not give the gas to Aunty Ifeoma because of their disagreements over Papa-Nnukwu, so she subtly suggests the delivery on her behalf. Mama must keep up the illusion that Papa is the benevolent protector of his family and she preys on this role to lobby for the desired outcome. Mama is not able to demand or even ask out right for what she wants. Over the years, she has learned that this is the only effective way to get something she needs.

Summary and Analysis of Chapter Eight

Summary

On their way to Nsukka, Jaja forgets when it is his time to recite the rosary. They pass burned out hulls of cars destroyed in accidents. Kevin, the driver, stops at a police checkpoint and hands over a bribe so they may pass. If Papa was in the car, he would allow them to search the car and check the family's papers; he would never participate in the corruption by bribing the police. They drive under a wide metal arch flanked by security guards. This is the entrance to the University of Nigeria, Nsukka, where Aunty Ifeoma teaches. The green lawn houses a statue of a lion standing on its hind legs. The school motto is inscribed underneath – "To restore the dignity of man."

They arrive at Aunty's flat. There is a sprawling garden filled with flowers on the front lawn. Aunty Ifeoma hugs them tightly when they get out of the car. Kevin presents Ifeoma with the gifts of food and gas cylinders. Aunty dances with joy. They enter her flat and Kambili is shocked at how low the ceilings are. The air smells of spices and kerosene. Aunty gives them a tour, showing them the room where she sleeps with Chima and the room Kambili will share with Amaka. Obiora sleeps in the living room, so Jaja will bunk with him there. When Kevin leaves, Kambili has the urge to run after him with her suitcase and ask him to take her back home.

Aunty's children come home and greet their cousins. Amaka is wearing lipstick and a tight dress. She barely hugs Kambili before pulling away. Obiora takes Jaja to the corner store to buy soft drinks. When he leaves, Kambili searches Jaja's eyes for the sense of bewilderment she is experiencing. Kambili follows Amaka to her room. Amaka is brusque as always, telling Kambili that Nsukka is not as happening as Enugu. She mentions two hotspots, assuming Kambili goes out all the time. Kambili manages to say no, again omitting the truth about her life.

Kambili turns away from Amaka when she strips to her underwear. She has been taught it is a sin to look upon another person's nakedness. Amaka gestures to a battered tape player at the foot of her bed and apologizes patronizingly that it is inferior to the sound system in Enugu. Amaka does not listen to American pop music, favoring culturally conscious Nigerian musicians. Everything is foreign to Kambili and Amaka looks at her as if she is a lab animal to be categorized.

Amaka helps her mother cook and Aunty Ifeoma informs Kambili and Jaja that they will be treated like guests for tonight only. Tomorrow they must pitch in. Aunty offers a quick prayer, unlike Papa's nightly mass. Supper is meager – a few pieces of chicken on mismatched plates. The kids speak authoritatively with their mother, teasing and joking. Dinner, too, is different from what Kambili is used to.

Amaka constantly teases Kambili when confronted with her cousins' lifestyle. Just like her classmates, Amaka assumes the luxury Kambili is accustomed to makes her feel big. But Kambili wishes she could disappear or at least apologize for whatever she has done to make Amaka upset. At dinner, the family takes their plates to the TV. Aunty Ifeoma tells Kambili and Jaja to join their cousins if they wish, allowing them to watch as much TV as they like. Jaja tells his aunt that they must follow their schedules and study. Aunty Ifeoma takes their schedules and puts them into her pocket. She tells them that while they are in her house, they are on holiday.

At prayers that evening, the family follows the rosaries with Igbo songs. Kambili and Jaja do not sing. The next morning, the kids get water from their local tap. Jaja joins in, reporting to his sister that he slept on a thin mattress next to Obiora. His voice is filled with wonder, not derision. At morning prayer, Aunty prays for the University but also that they may find peace and laughter that day. Kambili is surprised. The family takes turns bathing before breakfast. Aunty Ifeoma carefully rations each serving of powdered milk. Kambili thinks of the plentiful supply of cold milk in her refrigerator at home. Aunty Ifeoma hurries the kids through breakfast so they can tour the university and come home to prepare dinner for their guest, their friend Father Amadi.

On their way to the car, Jaja admires a purple hibiscus in Aunty's garden. He runs his finger over the beautiful petals. Aunty explains that they were created as an experiment by her botanist friend Phillipa. They tour the University in Aunty's beat-up car, coasting down hills to conserve the scarce fuel. Kambili notices each building she passes is worn and in disrepair. Aunty shows them the Institute of African Studies, where she teaches, and the hostels for female students. She points out one dorm in particular, where she says Amaka will launch her activist movements in college. Aunty Ifeoma says maybe Kambili will join her cousin. Kambili does not respond – if, where, and what she studies will be determined by Papa.

Aunty Ifeoma points out Odim Hill. She says that from its beautiful view, you can survey how God laid out the valleys and hills. Kambili's mind drifts to the white hands of God creating the landscape. They drive past the vice-chancellor's house, explaining that the hedges were recently trampled by rioting students. Obiora tells Jaja they were rioting because they had no light or water for a month. Amaka says that if she were vice-chancellor, her students would never be without utilities. Obiora challenges her, asking how it would be possible if a Big Man in capital city Abuja intercepted University funds. Kambili looks at Obiora, a year younger than herself, but yet so much bolder and assured.

Back in the flat, Kambili helps Amaka peel the large yams they brought from Enugu. Aunty Ifeoma tells Kambili that she will like Father Amadi. He is new to their local chaplaincy but already in demand by the villagers. Amaka says he connects with their family the most. Aunty Ifeoma teases her daughter, saying she is protective of the young priest. Amaka yells at Kambili for wasting yam and Kambili jumps, dropping the knife. Amaka jokes she should add learning to peel properly to her schedule. Aunty Ifeoma tells Amaka to go outside. Kambili is grateful for her aunt.

Father Amadi arrives wearing an earthy cologne. He is an attractive African man with a voice like a song. Kambili immediately takes comfort in his presence. But he makes her nervous as well. She remembers he once visited St. Agnes, following a sermon with an Igbo song ,to the displeasure of Papa. She remembers the song, too. Ifeoma and her children chatter through dinner, praising Papa, Ade Coker and the Standard for telling the truth. They talk about Aokpe, Amaka saying it was about time an apparition of the Virgin Mary appeared in Africa.

After dinner, Father Amadi leads the prayers and song. They watch Newsline together on the TV. Kambili looks up to see the priest's eyes on her. She suddenly has trouble swallowing. Father Amadi says he has not seen Kambili smile and laugh at all that day. She says nothing. Aunty Ifeoma explains that she is shy. Kambili excuses herself and goes to sleep, thinking of Father Amadi's voice.

Analysis

Aunty Ifeoma's family is markedly different than Papa's family. She banishes the children's schedules. In her house, they follow her rules. Aunty Ifeoma's authority is more respectful of her children and her relatives. Family depends on the interplay of each of its members. She encourages her children to question and to draw their own conclusions. Though she has lost her beloved husband, there is love in the home. Kambili and Jaja love their parents, but are not allowed to interact in any other mode outside of duty. Respect in Aunty Ifeoma's household is a two-way street. Kambili is shocked, but Jaja responds with wonder.

Kambili is somewhat shocked by the conditions in Aunty Ifeoma's flat. She notes its low ceilings and well-worn furniture when she arrives. The water can only be pumped once a day, they drink powdered milk, and Obiora sleeps in the living room. Kambili does not judge their economic situation though Amaka assumes she does. Rather, she is ashamed that she does not understand their way of life. This is the first taste of what life is like beyond the gated walls of her compound. She is a stranger to even the simplest task. Privilege is limiting for Kambili.

Amaka is derisive of her cousin but Kambili will not talk back. She has not been raised to justify or defend herself. Amaka only sees the Kambili's flaws and inabilities as markers of her cushy life. Kambili, of course, cannot tell her cousin the price she pays for the luxuries and that items like the stereo and satellite TV are simply illusions of wealth. At this point, Kambili suffers the wrath of her cousin while longing to be more like her. There is a bridge she can not yet cross.

Father Amadi is also a stark contrast with Father Benedict. As he explains in Chapter Ten, he joined the priesthood because it answered the most questions asked in his young life. Kambili assumes that all clergy must have a calling to a higher power, but she learns that there can be an intellectual as well as spiritual connection to God. His physical beauty inspires a crush but her affections are deepened by his gentle nature and the attention he pays her. He is a stimulus for her coming of age.

The religion observed by Ifeoma's family is less strict than Papa's version of Catholicism. Though Ifeoma is devout, she allows her children to question both the nature of faith and its uses in Africa. She prays that her family may find laughter, a completely foreign concept to Kambili. Furthermore, she prays that God look after Papa-Nnukwu even though he does not share their faith. Combined with the exuberant Igbo songs they sing after evening prayer, this freer iteration of Catholicism blends new and old traditions. Faith is a more fluid entity in their household.

Summary and Analysis of Chapter Nine

Summary

Kambili and Jaja share in the chores in Aunty Ifeoma's house. Kambili wishes her Aunt were there to speak for her when Amaka criticizes her. Amaka's friends visit and compliment Kambili on her long, natural hair. At first, Kambili does not realize they are speaking to her. Her cousin has to shout her name to get her attention. The next day, Kambili overhears Amaka asking her mother if she's sure Kambili and Jaja aren't abnormal. Aunty Ifeoma tells her daughter she can have her own opinions, but she must treat her family with respect. Kambili's hands shake.

Kambili reads a book from the veranda when the neighborhood children come over to play. She watches them as they run about in the garden. Obiora asks Jaja where his name comes from, as it is not Igbo. Jaja explains that his real name is Chukwuka. Aunty Ifeoma chimes in, telling Obiora "Ja-Ja" was the only thing he could say as a baby, so the nickname stuck. She likens him to Jaja of Opobo, who Obiora identifies as the stubborn king. Aunty Ifeoma corrects him, telling the story of the defiant king of the Opobo people who did not sell his soul to the British when Nigeria was colonized. Obiora shrugs, saying the British took over anyway. Jaja answers back, to the surprise of his sister. The British may have won the war, but they lost many battles.

Chima asks Jaja what happened to his little finger on his left hand. It is withered by abuse. Aunty Ifeoma answers quickly – he had an accident. Kambili knows the truth. When Jaja missed two questions on his catechism test before Communion, Papa took him upstairs and locked the door. Jaja has not used his finger since. Mama calls to tell her children that soldiers barged into the new offices of the Standard. Ade Coker is in custody again. When Papa calls later in the evening, he asks Aunty Ifeoma to keep Kambili and Jaja for a few extra days.

Every time the phone rings, Kambili is afraid that something happened to her father. Father Amadi comes for dinner and she can't help but stare at him. Each time he looks at her, though, she looks away. The family jokes about playing football that weekend, but Aunty Ifeoma is distant. She tells her family that Papa-Nnukwu is ill. Father Amadi's brows furrow. He suggests she brings her father home to Nsukka. He offers to give her emergency fuel stored in the chaplaincy for the journey to Abba. During prayer, Kambili wonders where Papa-Nnukwu will stay. She prays that her father will never find out she shared a room with a heathen.

When Aunty Ifeoma takes Obiora to Abba, Kambili sits on the veranda watching Jaja in the garden. Amaka's music blares from her bedroom. Kambili asks Jaja if they are abnormal. He looks up at her, asks what abnormal means and then resumes tending the flowers.

Papa-Nnukwu arrives in the afternoon. He prefers to sit on the floor in the living room. Since the doctors in the clinic are on strike, Aunty Ifeoma arranges for a house call that evening. Jaja remarks how skinny his grandfather has gotten since they've seen him. Kambili asks whether he is concerned Papa will find out. Jaja's brow is not knitted with worry like hers. She asks him if he told Aunty Ifeoma what happened to his finger. He answers simply – she asked, so he told her. Kambili is almost frightened by his tone. He cleans his aunt's car, his toes tapping to an Igbo song. She thanks him, using an Igbo term she uses with her own sons.

The medical lab staff is on strike too, so Aunty Ifeoma cannot get tests done on Papa-Nnukwu. He feels well enough to join them for dinner. Aunty Ifeoma buries his medicine in his food so he can stomach it. Amaka is pleased to have her grandfather around. They share a strong bond. Since Papa-Nnukwu doesn't speak English, they tease him lightly in their learned tongue. During dinner, the lights go out. The children implore Papa-Nnukwu to tell them a story.

At Chima's request, Papa-Nnukwu tells his family how the tortoise cracked his shell. During a famine, the animals gather. They are weakened by hunger. Lion's roar is but a thin whine and Tortoise can barely carry his shell. Only Dog looks well. He insists because his family eats feces, they are still healthy. Since the rest of the animals won't do what Dog does, they decide they must sacrifice their mothers to be eaten. Each week, a different mother gives up their life to feed the village. A few days before Dog's mother is to be killed, the village hears him wailing. He tells them his mother has died of disease. They cannot eat her. A few days later, Tortoise hears Dog calling his mother. A rope descends from the sky. Tortoise learns that Dog's mother is still alive, living in the sky with wealthy friends. Dog's health has not suffered because he has been eating all along. Tortoise schemes, telling Dog he must take him up to the sky or else he will tell the village the truth. Dog agrees. Soon after, Tortoise becomes greedy, wanting not only his portion but Dog's as well. Mimicking Dog, Tortoise asks for the rope to be lowered one day. Dog finds him and is furious. He calls to his mother and she cuts the rope. Tortoise lands on a pile of rocks and his shell is cracked to this day.

Analysis

Jaja's name, derived from a childhood nickname, is similar to a legendary king of ethnic Nigerians, Jaja of Opobo. He is known as the Defiant King. Before coming to Nsukka, Jaja is not defiant. He is shy and quiet for a seventeen-year-old boy, raised, as his father says, with the fear of God. Though he is denied the initiation rite, he begins to act like the defiant king. He says though the British won the war, the Opobo won many battles. He intends to win battles against his father.

Jaja's defiance begins to blossom in Nsukka. When the Obiora asks him about his deformed finger, Aunty Ifeoma responds quickly that it was an accident. She is clearly covering for him. Later, Kambili asks if Jaja told her about what had really happened. He says simply that she asked, so he told the truth. Neither Kambili or

Jaja are accustomed to telling the truth. They kept their father's secret of abuse.

Government corruption is a thread woven in this chapter. Military leadership has taken over the country following a coup. There is no democracy and the government does not respect the rights of the people. The government controls the university, forcing salary freezes. Access to fuel and food in Nsukka is limited. Even medical centers are on strike. Daily life is a struggle. Even Papa's business is suffering in this climate. Soldiers storm the new offices of the Standard. Threats of violence are used to intimidate people into order. Papa's actions can be viewed as a metaphor for the corrupt Head of State. He punishes his people by withholding and violence. Paradoxically, Papa believes in democracy.

While dining with Papa-Nnukwu, Obiora declares that morality is relative. This is an important point. Papa does not believe that morality is relative. For him, there is one true God and one true path leading to heaven. Obiora's family is more liberal and rational and they approach faith from a broader perspective. Their morality is determined by a more humanistic approach. Papa-Nnukwu, though of a different faith, is not turned away. For Mama, morality is relative as well. When she becomes aware of the severity of the abuse, Aunty Ifeoma cannot believe that she stays in Enugu. But Mama's experiences up to this point teach her that morality is synonymous with family. She is behaving as she always has within the family unit. When she finally comes around to putting a stop to the abuse, she poisons Papa. Even if Jaja had not taken the blame, Mama would not be considered a murderer. Her situation dictates a different code of morality.

Papa-Nnukwu shares the story of how the tortoise's shell was cracked. In Igbo legend, the tortoise is a trickster figure that deceives the other animals in the world. In this parable, the tortoise is punished for his greed. There is a parallel in this story to what is happening in Nigeria. Dog, or the government, is hoarding food during a famine. Dog lies about how he stays healthy, as the government misdirects funds into their own pockets. The greedy Tortoise aligns himself with Dog rather than telling the rest of the animals. If you are friends with those in power, no harm will come to you. Papa criticizes the papers that are soft on the inherent corruption and he also will not participate in standard bribes. When Kevin drives Kambili and Jaja to Nsukka, he bribes soldiers at a checkpoint – something he would never do if Papa were in the car. Tortoise represents those who profit from greed. When the children wonder who in the sky is feeding Dog, Obiora guesses that it is rich ancestors. By this he means that ancestors will protect their lineage. Just as the mothers of the other animals were willing to sacrifice themselves, Dog's mother and relatives were willing to lie for him. But they are not living up to their moral code. In the ritual that Papa-Nnukwu recites each morning, he says that he shares what little he has with those who have less.

Summary and Analysis of Chapter Ten

Summary

Father Amadi visits the next day and invites Obiora and Jaja to play football that evening. He tells Jaja to invite his sister, but when they leave in the evening, Kambili pretends to be asleep. She goes out to the living room to find Amaka tending to Papa-Nnukwu. Papa-Nnukwu tells Kambili that her cousin would have been chosen to decorate the shrines of their gods. Watching them, Kambili feels a longing for something she knows she will never have. She joins Aunty Ifeoma in the kitchen.

Aunty Ifeoma asks why Kambili is crying. But Kambili does not know herself. Aunty Ifeoma teaches Kambili how to prepare cocoyam. She says that Our Lady is watching over Papa-Nnukwu. Kambili is confused because he is a heathen. Aunty Ifeoma gently explains that he is not a heathen, but a traditionalist, and that sometimes what is unfamiliar is just as good. She tells her that when Papa-Nnukwu does his itu-nzu each morning, his declaration of innocence, it is the same as their repetition of the rosary.

The next morning, Aunty Ifeoma wakes Kambili before dawn. She tells her to observe Papa-Nnukwu's morning ritual. She sits quietly on the veranda and watches him draw lines on the ground in clay, giving thanks for the sunrise. He draws another line and offers his innocence. With a third line, he says he has tried to help others who have nothing with the little that he has. He prays for the curse to be lifted from Papa and for the children of his children to be blessed and steered away from evil. He rises to stretch and Kambili sees his naked body. She does not look away. He is smiling deeply when he enters the house. Kambili never smiles when she says the rosary.

Amaka decides to paint a portrait of Papa-Nnukwu on the veranda in order to catch the sunlight on his skin. Aunty Ifeoma asks Kambili to help her prepare orah leaves, but she does not know how. The task falls to Amaka and she is angry. Aunty Ifeoma asks Kambili why she does not talk back to her cousin. Finally, Kambili's voice rises above a whisper. She tells Amaka that there is no need to shout. If she teaches her how to prepare the orah, she will do it. Amaka laughs. She says she did not think Kambili's voice could be this loud.

Father Amadi comes for dinner. He holds Kambili's hand longer than the others'. Kambili learns that he will soon be leaving. Papa-Nnukwu asks where he will be going and Aunty Ifeoma says he is a missionary and will go where he is told to go. Papa-Nnukwu wonders aloud why an African will go to the white man's land to convert others. Obiora says that religion and oppression often go hand in hand. Father Amadi teases Obiora, calling him mad. Amaka laughs. Father Amadi looks to Kambili who says nothing. He praises her for not picking fights that cannot be won. He tells her he will take her to play football. Amaka looks at her cousin – she is terrified.

Amaka lends Kambili a pair of shorts, but she does not spend time lingering in the mirror. At home, she and Jaja look at themselves only long enough to make sure their buttons are done properly. In Father Amadi's car, her eyes fall on his muscular thighs. She listens to his lilting voice. She blurts out that she sleeps in the same room with a heathen. Father Amadi asks why she considers this a sin. Because Papa told her so. Father Amadi says Jaja has told him about Papa. She wonders what her brother has said.

At the stadium, Father Amadi tells Kambili to catch him. She runs after him, but he is too fast. He tells her she has legs for running. She can't smile although she wants to. Father Amadi looks at a red stain on her hand. Lipstick. He asks if she has ever worn it before. Kambili says no, and an amused and embarrassed smile creeps over her lips. She watches him play football with some local boys, touching the tank top he has peeled off before the game.

In the car, they listen to Igbo songs and he tells Kambili that the boys inspire him. He wonders why she hasn't asked him any questions. Amaka is all questions. Kambili laughs in spite of herself. She asks him why he became a priest. He says his path to the priesthood was a lot more complicated than simply following a calling. The priesthood came closest to answering the many questions he had in his youth. He drops her off at her aunt's house. Her chest is filled with a lightness for the first time.

Aunty Ifeoma tells Kambili that Papa has called. Someone from the village told him that Papa-Nnukwu was staying with them. Irate, he insists on picking them up the next day. But, Aunty Ifeoma convinces Papa to let them stay an extra day. She also tells Kambili that Papa managed to get Ade Coker released from prison.

When the family wakes the next morning, they find that Papa-Nnukwu has died. Jaja covers his body with his wrapper. Kambili wants to touch her grandfather, but she knows Papa would be outraged. She looks away so she will not have to lie if Papa asks if Jaja has touched him. Later, Aunty Ifeoma asks if Kambili had seen Papa-Nnukwu's face. He was smiling in death. Amaka is irate. She says he would still be alive if the clinic was not on strike. Kambili wishes she could hug her cousin or cry loudly with her, but she stays still. Jaja tries to comfort her, but Amaka throws his arm off her shoulder.

Papa arrives during dinner though he had promised his children could stay an extra day. Aunty Ifeoma tells him their father has died. He does not cry, but asks her if she called a priest and offers to pay for a Catholic funeral. Ifeoma refuses angrily. She retreats to her bedroom, sobbing. Papa tells Kambili and Jaja to pack their bags. When Aunty Ifeoma hugs them goodbye, she returns their schedules. Kambili asks her to say goodbye to Father Amadi. Chima is upset; he does not want Jaja to go. Papa offers Aunty Ifeoma money to buy him a gift. Amaka shoves a parcel wrapped in plastic into Kambili's hand and then turns away quickly. It is her painting of

Papa-Nnukwu. Kambili hides it in her suitcase.

Mama is waiting for them at the door, her face swollen with a black eye. Jaja tells
her that Papa-Nnukwu is dead. Papa is angry with his sister for not calling a priest.
Jaja says that maybe he didn't want to convert. Mama tries to quickly cover her son's
disrespect, but it is too late. The dinner prayers are longer than usual as Papa asks to
cleanse his children's sin of omission. Jaja asks Papa for the key to his room. Papa is
shocked – only he is allowed to lock their doors. Jaja only wants privacy, but Papa
assumes he will sin against himself. Later, Mama asks Kambili if it is feels different
to be back. Kambili says yes, thinking there is too much empty space in their home.

Papa summons Kambili from the living room. She goes upstairs and to the bathroom
where he is waiting. She climbs into the tub and he pours boiling water onto her feet
from a teapot. He tells her she is precious and that she should not just walk into sin.
If she does, she burns her feet. Kambili cries and screams I'm sorry. She is afraid to
move even after the water stops running. Mama appears and lifts her to her room.

Mama gives Kambili pain relievers and spreads a salve of salt and cold water onto
her feet. When she leaves, Kambili hobbles over to the painting Amaka gave her.
She doesn't dare unwrap in but she touches it fondly, thinking of her cousins and of
Father Amadi. When she gets back in bed, Papa appears and tells her that everything
he does is for her sake. He tells her he was once caught masturbating and his priest
put his hand in boiling water. Papa was happy for the pain, for he never sinned
against himself again.

Jaja comes into Kambili's room the next day, wearing the same thick, padded socks.
His feet are burned as well. She shows him the painting, still in its wrapper, and he
takes her downstairs. In the fridge, he has hidden a stalk of purple hibiscus from
Aunty Ifeoma's garden. Though Papa has given him permission to plant the flowers
in their garden, Jaja still replaces it quickly when he hears him coming.

Over lunch, Papa complains about the price of pagan funerals. Kambili is surprised
to learn that he has offered to pay for Papa-Nnukwu's service. Ade Coker and
another man interrupts dinner with important Standard business. He has been offered
an exclusive interview with the Head of State, Big Oga, in exchange for their silence
on pro-democracy activist Nwankiti Ogechi. Ade insists he is being bought off and
that the government is trying to cover up the disappearance and murder of Ogechi.
The man with Ade stresses that they should wait to publish their story on Ogechi.
Ade is adamant they report the truth. The three men retire to Papa's study. Later that
night, government officials come to the Achike home to offer Papa a truckload of
cash as a bribe. He waves them off his property.

The next day's issue of the Standard leads with a story on Ogechi. They quote from
an anonymous source who claims that Ogechi had been shot and his body covered in
acid to melt the flesh off of his bones. They have killed him twice. From radio
reports, the family learns that Nigeria is suspended from the Commonwealth,

admonished by Canada and Holland for the murder of Ogechi. That night, and every other night to follow, democratic supporters come to Papa for advice. He warns them to be careful and inspect their cars for bombs. Papa's hands shake each night at dinner. Jaja comforts a worried Aunty Ifeoma when she calls, telling her Papa is too connected to prominent foreign men to be harmed.

Kambili takes the phone from Jaja, and tells her aunt to greet Father Amadi for her. Kambili speaks to Amaka, who has a more breezy tone. Kambili thanks her for the painting. They speak of Papa-Nnukwu's funeral the following week. Amaka hopes that Kambili and Jaja can come out for Easter, planning the pilgrimage they did not take to Aokpe. Amaka's Confirmation is scheduled for Easter as well, and she would like her cousins to be there. During her studies, she writes Father Amadi's name over and over again. When school resumes, she joins her classmates' volleyball games. She does not notice their taunts of backyard snob. She thinks only of Father Amadi.

Analysis

Papa-Nnukw is a powerful force in Kambili and Jaja's lives. Although they are not able to spend enough time with him to know him fully, he touches both of their lives in different ways. For Jaja, Papa-Nnukwu represents masculinity. At Christmas, Papa-Nnukwu compliments Jaja's wisdom, telling him that he is his own father who has come back. For the Igbo, who believe in reincarnation, this is high praise. Jaja does not shy away from his grandfather like Kambili does. Through him, he understands his ancestry. Kambili moves gingerly around Papa-Nnukwu, afraid to incur the wrath of Papa. But Aunty Ifeoma shows her a different side to the "heathens" that Papa despises. Kambili watches the full ritual and sees her grandfather's nakedness. Having seen no godlessness in his eyes at Christmas, she sees no sin in his innocence here. The joy on his face opens something up in Kambili. Through Papa-Nnukwu, she understands that faith can fulfill a person and not just be used as a rod of discipline.

Kambili's first outing with Father Amadi marks the beginning of her mild sexual awakening. Though she does not know how to play football, he tries to engage her by telling her to catch him. He speaks of Jesus and sings in Igbo. He is a clash of ideas in an attractive man. The attention he pays Kambili is at first frightening but she begins to see herself from his eyes. She also trades her long skirt for a pair of Amaka's forbidden shorts. And she even wears red lipstick for the first time. Father Amadi is playful and, when he notes the lipstick rubbed off on her hand, she finally smiles. There is a release of the tension with which she has always lived. The world does not end when she puts on shorts and lipstick. Kambili's questioning of her father's rules are much more subtle and personal. Later she confesses her crush to Amaka, but for Kambili, her affection is both deeper and more innocent.

The increasing pressure the government places on Papa takes its toll. Ade Coker is arrested again and released again, thanks to Papa's involvement. Knowing that the interview with the Head of State's office is a trick to get them off the trail of the murdered activist, the Standard runs their story anyway. Papa will not be bribed. Even though they know the risks, they proceed. There is an echo to this behavior in Jaja's defiance. Jaja asks for the key to his room even though he knows he will likely be reprimanded for it. There is a truth that must be told by both Papa and Jaja.

Things are different for Kambili. There is too much space at home. When she first steps foot in Aunty Ifeoma's flat, she is surprised at how meager the surroundings are. But as her life begins to open up, she no longer cares about the size of the flat, the water that can only be pumped once a day, or the kerosene cooker. Kambili sees the luxurious space at home for what it is – emptiness. When she gets back to school, she participates in sports though she is always picked last. There is a new silence now, the silencing of the schoolyard taunts. She only hears Father Amadi's voice, giving her the confidence to face her detractors. Even in this short trip, Kambili's growth is monumental. A simple volleyball game may not seem like a giant leap, but Kambili is participating in the world around her and allowing herself to do something she wants to do. It is a step towards independence.

Jaja changes as well. He openly challenges his father when he criticizes Aunty Ifeoma for not calling a priest for Papa-Nnukwu. Jaja's tongue has come loose and he will not be quieted. After their feet are burned, Jaja visits Kambili. Kambili shows him the painting of Papa-Nnukwu and Jaja shows her the purple hibiscus. Both the painting and the flowers are symbols of their burgeoning independence. They are kept under wraps for now, but pieces of Nsukka have been brought into Enugu and it is only a matter of time before they emerge for good.

Summary and Analysis of Chapter Eleven

Summary

It rained heavily the day Ade Coker dies. He is killed at his table when he opens a package bomb. His daughter was sitting across from him, next to his wife and baby son. The package bore the seal of the State House. Kambili and Jaja come home from school to find Papa crumpled on the living room couch, sobbing. Jaja comforts him by saying Ade's death was God's will. Papa arranges for Ade's funeral and sets up trusts for Yewande and her children. He awards bonuses to his staff at the Standard, asking them to take long leaves. Kambili is wracked by nightmares of her father blowing up across from her at their table.

Weeks later, Papa still carries the heavy burden of his editor's death. Soldiers take a carton of dead rats to one of his factories to incur a health violation. The factory is shut down and Papa rarely visits his other factories. Papa also checks in on the children less frequently, so Jaja and Kambili take advantage of their looser schedules. Jaja visits with Kambili and asks to see the painting of Papa-Nnukwu. Papa is with Father Benedict, he explains, so there is nothing to fear. He runs his deformed finger over the paint as if in a trance. They sit and stare at the painting for a long time, long enough for Papa's visit to draw to a close.

Papa finds his children with the painting. Jaja claims ownership, but Kambili says it belongs to her. Papa asks if they have converted to heathen ways, then sways from side to side in rage. He grabs the painting and begins to tear it to pieces. Kambili shrieks and then falls on to the fragments to protect them. She does not get up when Papa tells her to. She curls up into the fetal position. Papa begins to kick her, rambling about damnation. He does not stop until Mama begs him to. Kambili passes out.

Kambili wakes up in the hospital, her entire body enflamed with pain. She hears fragments of phrases – broken rib, heal nicely, internal bleeding. Papa's eyes, soft in tears, hover over her. He promises nothing will happen to her. Father Benedict gives her extreme unction, though Mama insists she is fine. Kambili asks her to call Aunty Ifeoma.

Kambili, sedated, drifts in and out of consciousness. She thinks she dreams of Father Amadi's face, but he is in the room with Aunty Ifeoma. Kambili can't smile or speak. Aunty Ifeoma tells Mama that she must put a stop to what is happening. She insists that Kambili and Jaja come to Nsukka when Kambili is released from the hospital. Mama says Papa will never agree, but Aunty Ifeoma won't hear it. Before she falls asleep, Mama tells Kambili that Papa has been sick with worry. Kambili turns her head away from her mother.

A white Sister comes to the hospital to tutor Kambili. Kambili is surprised that she speaks Igbo as well as English. The Sister is wise. She knows that Kambili pretends to be in more pain than she is when the doctor examines her. Mother Lucy herself administers Kambili's exams and brings her report card. Kambili is first in her class.

Kambili's classmates visit, thinking she had survived an accident. In the hospital, the girls are friendlier. Chinwe gossips with her as if they had always been close. When they are alone, Ezinne asks Kambili if she will stop running away from home. Kambili says nothing. She is released two days later. Aunty Ifeoma convinces Papa to let her come to Nsukka.

Analysis

This is a chapter marked by extreme violence. The death of Ade Coker and Kambili's savage beating are both products of corruption. Ade is murdered by his own government and Kambili is nearly killed by her own father – two entities that are supposed to protect. Kambili dreams about Ade's body. Sometimes she dreams that Papa has been blown up in front of her. This is a shocking dream for a child to have, but her own experience with violence makes these images commonplace. Like Kambili's dream, the environment also reflects the drama in Purple Hibiscus. The day of Ade Coker's death is a day of great rains. This symbolizes the sadness and violence in the wake of his murder.

The painting is unwrapped, finally. This is a point of no return for the Achike children. Kambili knows that Papa can come upstairs at any moment, and yet they continue to stare at it. The painting is like Mama's figurines, in that it offers a respite from reality. However, the painting is loaded and looking upon it is an act of defiance. Jaja runs his deformed finger over the painting, a finger he never uses consciously. The painting has almost a healing effect on the children. Having confronted the true story at Aunty Ifeoma's flat, Jaja no longer hides his finger.

Jaja tries to protect his sister by claiming ownership of the painting. When she gets her period and is caught eating cereal, the entire family takes their share of punishment for abetting her sin. But here Kambili throws herself on the scraps and, in doing so, protects her family. Jaja and Mama are unharmed. Like the mothers in Papa-Nnukwu's Tortoise parable, Kambili sacrifices herself for her family.

Kambili becomes more willful after her ordeal. She turns her head away from her mother when she speaks of Papa's remorse. She also lies to the doctor, pretending to be weaker than she is so she will not have to go home. She does not challenge the lie that has been crafted for the sake of her classmates – that she has tried to run away from home. Typically, these lies are told to spare Papa's image from the truth. But, in a way, there is truth in Kambili running away. This lie places the blame on to Kambili in the eyes of her friend, but the root is the same as the truth. Looking at the painting of Papa-Nnukwu was dissent and escape.

The white sister who tutors Kambili at the hospital is similar to Father Amadi. She is European-born but is fluent in Igbo. The white sisters at Kambili's school never speak Igbo and even refrain from reciting the Nigerian pledge and anthem. Father Amadi melds practices from his homeland and his adopted religion as this sister has chosen to learn language of the country she lives in. These characters represent grace to Kambili as well as a more complicated and ambiguous perspective. The sister, who is complicit in Kambili's lies - even though lying is a sin – represents the sliding scale of morality that Obiora speaks of. Part of Kambili's journey is accepting that the world is more complex than it appears.

Summary and Analysis of Chapter Eleven

Summary and Analysis of Chapter Twelve

Summary

Kambili and Jaja arrive in Nsukka. Obiora and Chima are delicate with Kambili, offering to carry her bag or prepare a mango for her. Aku, winged termites, swarm in the backyard. Neighboring children run outside to catch them so they can be fried as a snack. Mature Obiora goes outside merely to observe; he does not get caught up in the revelry. He tells his mother he was never a child. Amaka laughs, then joins Kambili on the veranda. There is an ease to their relationship now. Amaka tells Kambili that she has become Father Amadi's sweetheart. Amaka lightly teases Kambili, who confirms her crush on the priest. Amaka says every girl on campus is in love with Father Amadi, but it is only Kambili he is concerned with. Amaka asks if Papa is responsible for Kambili's "illness." Kambili says yes.

Father Amadi comes to check in on Kambili. He gives her a warm hug that Kambili finds tense and delicious. Kambili wishes she were alone with Father Amadi. She sits and listens to his comforting voice.

The next day, Kambili wakes last and finds Aunty Ifeoma sitting on the veranda with a friend. The woman is a professor, like Aunty Ifeoma, but humorless. They discuss the University's decision to appoint a sole administrator that would displace the elected vice-chancellor. Aunty Ifeoma's friend says there is a list circulating with the names of disloyal professors. Ifeoma's name is on the list. She says she is not paid to be loyal, but to speak the truth. Her friend asks if the truth will feed her children. Kambili asks Amaka and Obiora what they are discussing. Amaka says her mother is in danger of being fired. Obiora says they will go to America if that happens. This distresses Amaka, who does not want to leave Nigeria. Kambili does not want to think of her family leaving Nsukka.

Kambili attends a football game with Father Amadi. She realizes that he speaks to his players like Aunty Ifeoma speaks to her children. They set goals for the children, encouraging them to jump higher. The goals are met because the children believe they can reach them. Kambili realizes she and Jaja excel only because they are terrified of what will happen if they fail. A dark cloud appears over Kambili. She tells Father Amadi what is on her mind and he tells her that he needs to believe in those boys so he can put his faith into something he does not question. He puts his hand on her hair and Kambili wishes she could lean her whole body against his.

Students riot in Nsukka the next morning. At least 500 people march in the streets, calling for the sole administrator to be ousted. Aunty Ifeoma assures the children that they are safe, but she turns off the lights so their flat does not draw attention. Later, Aunty Ifeoma learns that the sole administrator's house had been set on fire. Six university cars were torched as well. The university is shut down until further notice.

During Kambili's nap, she dreams the sole administrator is pouring hot water over Aunty Ifeoma's feet. When she jumps out of the bathtub, she jumps into America.

That evening, four soldiers barge into Aunty Ifeoma's flat. They tell the family they have been ordered to search the flat for documentation linking Aunty Ifeoma to the rioters. The soldiers ransack the apartment, scattering contents of drawers without looking through them. Obiora tries to stand up to them, but his mother tells him not to fight. The soldiers warn Ifeoma to be careful. Obiora says they should go to the police but his mother smiles. They are all working together. Obiora says it is time to leave for America, but Amaka yells at him. Running away will not solve problems. She urges that they stay and help fix their broken country. Obiora sneers at her. Aunty Ifeoma snaps at her quarreling children, ordering them to help clean up the mess.

The next morning, Kambili finds an earthworm in the shower. Though Obiora is fascinated with them, she removes it with a stick and throws it into the toilet. She joins Aunty Ifeoma in the kitchen and is served a glass of homemade soy milk. Aunty Ifeoma can no longer afford cow's milk. One of Ifeoma's students arrives with a chicken, a symbol of her engagement. The student will get married instead of returning to university when it opens. Jaja offers to kill the chicken even though he has never slaughtered an animal before. Kambili watches her brother slit the chicken's throat. A cold, clinical precision emerges in his actions. As he plucks the feathers, Jaja tells Kambili that he wants to leave with Aunty Ifeoma when she goes to America.

Father Amadi arrives to take Kambili to have her hair plaited. He takes her to Mama Joe, a friend of Aunty Ifeoma's. Father Amadi excuses himself and Mama Joe asks what his connection is to Kambili. Mama Joe is disappointed that he is a priest – all that maleness wasted. Like Amaka, Mama Joe insists that no man takes a girl to have her hair plaited unless he is interested in her. Kambili does not know what to say, so she watches a large snail escape from a bucket only to be replaced by Mama Joe. Father Amadi picks Kambili up when her hair is finished. He compliments her and tells her she should try out for the part of Our Lady in his church's play. Kambili says she cannot act. Father Amadi tells her she can do anything she wants.

Analysis

Shortly after Kambili and Jaja arrive in Nsukka, the aku – winged termites – begin to fly. Aunty Ifeoma jokes that although these insects are just matured versions of the termites considered to be pests, the neighborhood children go crazy for them. There is a sense of wonder and innocence in the aku. Chima is excited but Obiora merely goes outside to "observe." When Amaka teases him, he announces that he has never been a child. Obiora has been initiated into manhood by both the Igbo ritual and the death of his father. Obiora's coming of age has been accelerated by tragedy. The winged aku represent maturity and the freedom that it can inspire.

Kambili and Jaja also continue to mature. Like Jaja with his finger, Kambili decided it is time to start telling the truth about her own pain. When Amaka asks her if Papa is responsible for her illness, Kambili says yes. However, she does not want to discuss it because she sees no way out of her situation. She does not look back for Amaka's reaction. That, too, is a sign of maturity. Before she was concerned with what her cousin thought of her but now Kambili does not feel the need to please her. This only deepens their bond.

But not all is well in Nsukka. Students riot against the sole administrator because they have been without water and power. The rioting university students throw Aunty Ifeoma's situation into sharp relief. Obiora says that the university has become a microcosm of Nigeria with the sole administrator acting as Head of State. When the soldiers raid her flat, Aunty Ifeoma realizes that the situation is direr than she thought. Later, Kambili dreams that the sole administrator is pouring water over Aunty Ifeoma's feet. To the university, Aunty Ifeoma's sympathy towards her students is the sin that she has walked in. When she jumps out of the bathtub, she is in America. For Kambili this is a nightmare. While she does not want to see her aunt abused, she does not want to be abandoned by someone she loves.

When a chicken is brought to Aunty Ifeoma's flat, Jaja decides that he will kill it. This is his sacrifice. Although he has never slaughtered an animal before, the other children do not make fun of him and he does not ask how to proceed. Kambili goes with him and watches him slit its throat. He does not hesitate. Here he takes up the mantle of provider. Jaja also does not hesitate in telling Kambili that he wants to go to America with his cousins. Crossing an ocean is the only way to escape his father's reign.

Kambili's hair has not been plaited for some time. When she was in the hospital, Mama was unable to fix her hair because it caused her daughter too much pain. Father Amadi decides to take her himself. Mama's inability to plait her daughter's hair is symbolic of her inability to take care of her daughter. Kambili is told that only men who have affection for girls take them to get their hair plaited. Here, Kambili is transferring some of her dependencies from her Mama to a man she likes. This can be seen as a metaphor for coming of age as well. A ritual of comfort and familial duty takes on a sexualized overtone.

Summary and Analysis of Chapter Thirteen

Summary

Kambili and Amaka attend mass at St. Peter's, Father Amadi's chaplaincy. It is less ornate than St. Agnes, and the congregation is dressed more casually than those who assemble at Kambili's church. Kambili nearly swoons when she receives communion from Father Amadi. He drives the girls home and reminds Amaka to choose her confirmation name by the following day. She is stubborn, insisting she does not want an English name. He offers to help her choose.

Kambili sits on the veranda with her aunt and her friend Chiaku. They discuss university politics. The son of one of the professors stole his father's test answers to sell to his students. Since the university closed, the students have harassed the boy for their money to be returned. The professor beats his son for the theft. Chiaku friend says they are trying to treat the symptom and not the cause. If the professors can't afford food, they cannot blame their children for stealing. Beating the boy will not put an end to the tyranny. Chiaku tells Aunty Ifeoma about her time in Cambridge, where she was treated as a second-class citizen. She warns Ifeoma that she will face the same fate in America. She echoes Amaka's desire to address the problems at home rather than run away. Obiora interrupts, defending his mother. Chiaku leaves soon after and Aunty Ifeoma punishes her son for the disrespect. Amaka squeezes Kambili's hand and calls her brother stupid for wanting to leave Nigeria.

The power outages have spoiled the majority of the meat in the refrigerator. Kambili and Amaka pick stones out of rice on the veranda. They listen to Amaka's tapes of Fela and Onyeka. Kambili has never felt such companionship. Without warning, Mama shows up. She emerges from a taxi, unsteady. Aunty Ifeoma ushers her inside and asks what happened. Papa broke a table over Mama's stomach, not knowing she was pregnant. The beating causes another miscarriage. When released from the hospital, she took a cab straight to Nsukka.

Aunty Ifeoma does not let Mama come to the phone when Papa calls. But when she insists on calling him back, Mama reports that Papa will pick up his family the following day. Aunty Ifeoma is incredulous. Mama says that Papa has been under enormous strain since Ade's death and the shuttering of his factory. When Aunty Ifeoma pushes her, Mama asks her where she would go if she left Enugu. She dismisses Ifeoma's suggestion to move out as "university talk."

Papa comes the next day. Kambili is surprised to see how thin he has grown in the last few weeks. His entire face is covered with a pimply rash. When Kambili hugs Amaka goodbye, she calls her me nwanne m nwanyi – my sister. In the car, Jaja will not look at Kambili. She wants to tell him with her eyes how much she wishes to be in Nsukka at Easter. When they arrive home, the gates are opened and Kambili is nauseated by the overwhelming smell of ripening cashews, mangos and avocados. Jaja points to his purple hibiscus about to bloom.

The next Sunday is Palm Sunday. Jaja does not go to communion and Papa throws his missal at him.

Analysis

Aunty Ifeoma's argument with Chiaku is a metaphor for what is happening in the country. The professor whose son sold test answers is chided for trying to solve the symptom and not the real illness – corruption. When Aunty Ifeoma defends her choice of moving to America against her friend's bitterness, Obiora interrupts them. Here, he takes his maturity too far. He is still a child and is reprimanded for his disrespect. Challenging authority is expected but there is a price to be paid if one exceeds his or her limits.

The example of the father and his boy and also Obiora's punishment can be contrasted with the punishment inflicted on Kambili and Jaja. There is a difference between discipline and cruelty. Amaka explains to Kambili that being flogged by Aunty Ifeoma is not pleasant, but the discussion that ensues afterwards is even worse. Aunty Ifeoma uses corporal punishment as a corrective, but then discusses openly why she was provoked to such a degree that warrants the switch. Papa explains his intention, but the method is so severe that pain and fear become the lesson. Aunty Ifeoma tries to explain this to Mama when she turns up battered.

Amaka's reluctance to choose a confirmation name is indicative of her uneasiness with colonialism. In Roman Catholicism, there are seven sacraments, three of which are rites of initiation – Baptism, Eucharist and Confirmation. Baptism is performed at birth by anointing a child's head with holy water. The Eucharist, or receiving of communion, is to be nourished by Jesus through the ingestion of his "body" in the form of a wafer. Confirmation is completed by teenagers at the age of fifteen. Young men and women are anointed with oil and choose a confirmation name, typically the name of a saint. Though it is largely a symbolic gesture, Amaka does not want to give up her Nigerian identity.

Amaka calls Kambili her sister in this chapter. This signifies their bond and also echoes Aunty Ifeoma's use of "my wife" when referring to Mama. Family is forged not only by blood but also by connection and camaraderie. The titles connote the feelings that cannot be conveyed in simple terms. The women in the Achike umunna flout conventional familial titles to flout patriarchy.

Nature takes on symbolic meaning at the end of this chapter. When Kambili and Jaja return to Enugu, Kambili is overwhelmed by the sickeningly sweet scent of rotting fruit. Cashews, avocado and mangos litter the ground and give off this cloying order. Kambili used to delight in the vast backyard, daydreaming while looking outside her window. However, when she returns from Nsukka each time, the luxuries she has grown accustomed to take on a darker shade. Here, the fruits that symbolize status are rotting just as the Achike family is rotting. But Jaja's purple hibiscus - his rebellion – is about to bloom.

This chapter concludes with Palm Sunday and the book comes full circle back to the beginning. The first three parts of the book are a told in flashback with the forth part indicated as the present. Breaking Gods refers to Palm Sunday, when Papa's thrown missal breaks Mama's figurines. The title takes on another meaning, as Jaja's refusal to partake in mass is his "break" with God. The second section, which concludes here, is called Speaking With Our Spirits. This section charts the coming of age stories of both Kambili and Jaja who are forced to speak only through gesture and actions. As this section unfolds in flashback, the scenes flow like memory. Kambili, as the narrator, is choosing which memories are the most crucial in explaining what happens on Palm Sunday. This puts the story squarely in the point of view of Kambili and we can glimpse how she has changed by how she describes certain events. For instance, in this chapter, Kambili focuses on the card games she lost rather than her inevitable return to Enugu. Having distance from this night, she is able to point to her train of thought as evidence of her growth in confidence. Instead of dreaming of pain or fretting about her punishment, she reminisces about time spent with her cousin. This is a detail that Kambili, speaking from three years beyond this night, identifies as important.

Summary and Analysis of Chapter Thirteen

Summary and Analysis of Chapter Fourteen

PART THREE – THE PIECES OF GODS: AFTER PALM SUNDAY

Summary

Everything comes tumbling down after Palm Sunday. A fierce wind uproots several frangipani trees, the satellite dish dislodges from the roof, and Sisi breaks a full set of Mama's plates. Everyone changes. Mama speaks above a whisper and no longer sneaks food to Jaja when he doesn't come down for dinner. She carries his meals to him on trays. Kambili doesn't know how to react to the new, brittle air in the house. Through dinner, she stares at the portrait of her Grandfather and closes her eyes during prayer. Jaja does not leave his room and at first barricades his door with his desk. Papa, whose rashes have gotten worse, cannot get in.

Yewande Coker visits with her children. Her daughter spoke her first word that morning and she praises Papa for sending her to the best doctors in Nigeria. Papa, in turn, praises God and will not accept Yewande's thanks. Kambili relays the story to Jaja, thanking God for the girl's voice. But Jaja looks at her askew. He says the girl will never heal. When she leaves, Kambili easily pushes the desk aside. She wonders why Papa was unable to move it.

Kambili dreads Easter Sunday. She knows Jaja will not go. Papa's hands shake violently during breakfast, so he decides the family will attend evening mass. Aunty Ifeoma calls and tells Kambili that she has been terminated by the university. She has applied for a visa from the American embassy. Father Amadi has received notice as well and he will leave for Germany at the end of the month. Jaja tells Papa that he and Kambili will leave for Nsukka immediately to spend Easter with their cousins. Too weak to argue, Papa allows them to go. They pack hastily. Kambili goes into her father's room. He is disheveled, but he hugs her and kisses her forehead.

Aunty Ifeoma's apartment is swelteringly hot. The children cook over their kerosene cooker. Obiora says there is no need to save the gas cylinders, as they won't be in Nigeria for much longer. Amaka shakes her head. Their mother does not have her visa yet. Kambili waits on the veranda until the cooker stops smoking, then she helps prepare and serve supper. Amaka tells Kambili that the intense sun is a warning for rain. Papa-Nnukwu taught her about the angry sun. She reminisces about helping her mother deter thieves at the university and sighs. Amaka does not want to go to America. Kambili tries to comfort her. At least there will be fresh milk in bottles. Amaka smiles at her cousin.

The skies open up and the children gather rainwater in buckets. Father Amadi visits. Amaka and Obiora tease him about his assignment to Germany. They wonder if, since the white men brought their white God to Africa, perhaps Father Amadi can repackage God to bring to Germany. Father Amadi smiles and shakes his head. In Europe, there are no indigenous cultures that need to be pacified. Father Amadi looks to Kambili's troubled face. She does not know what will happen. In two weeks, school starts again. By then, Aunty Ifeoma may be gone. Jaja refuses to speak to Papa. Even though she wants to speak to him, Kambili refuses as well.

They speak in the garden. Kambili plucks flowers and places the petals on her fingers, Father Amadi dangerously close. He tells her he will go to Enugu the following week to talk to Father Benedict. He will recommend that Kambili and Jaja go to boarding school. He reassures her but she looks away. He asks her to look at him. His brown eyes nearly make her swoon. Father Amadi slips a petal off of her finger and holds her hand. That night, she bathes in the rainwater. She does not heat the water for fear that it will lose the smell of the sky. She does not wash her left hand, where Father Amadi had slipped the petal off of her finger. And she does not remove the earthworms from the shower. She lets them slide away with the water.

Analysis

The most striking development in this chapter is Mama's defiance. Instead of hiding her actions – feeding Jaja in his room, giving orders to the staff – she finds her voice. There are two reasons why this happens. She is inspired by Jaja and is willing to protect him by siding with him. And, as revealed in the next chapters, she is poisoning Papa. She knows that he is weak and cannot challenge her.

Amaka does not want to go to America. Her home is in Nigeria. Although politically problematic, she does not want to abandon her country: she wants to stay and try to fight injustices. Aunty Ifeoma's friend Phillipa has gone to America and is supposedly happy, but her other friend Chiaku remembers her time in Europe. She felt like an animal on display. Aunty Ifoema has no choice after she gets fired. If she cannot feed her children, she must consider other options. Though leaving her home is not the most desired outcome, she feels she must. The Achike family's story parallels its greater context of political unrest, and vice versa. Mama does not want to leave her home so, like Amaka, she desires to fix the problems in her own house. Her murder of Papa can be viewed as a coup.

When the family finds out that Father Amadi is assigned to Germany, Obiora and Amaka engage him in a discussion about colonialism. They suggest that since the white men brought their white man to Africa, perhaps Father Amadi should "repackage" his God for Europe's consumption. Obiora is suggesting Father Amadi disseminate a black image of God. In the final chapter of the book, Amaka tells Kambili that academics dispute the apparition in Aokpe because God wouldn't come to Africa. Aunty Ifeoma's children are challenging the dominant Western belief system. Father Amadi jokes that there are no indigenous cultures in Europe that need to be pacified. Religion was a tool used by imperialists to more easily colonize Africa. Missionaries taught Africans about their view of sin and morality in order to keep them in line. Eroding the indigenous culture is the first step towards assimilation. As a traditionalist, Papa-Nnukwu sought to preserve his own culture. His bond with Amaka makes her question her own faith. The difficulty in choosing a confirmation name is indicative of her challenge to colonialism.

The last paragraph of this chapter is a beautiful description of Kambili's growth as illustrated through her reaction to several environmental factors. First, she does not want to wash her hand for fear of washing off the memory of Father Amadi. The water she uses is unadulterated rainwater, unheated to retain the scent of the sky. She wants to carry nature with her. The rains have fallen after an extreme heat, symbolizing the relief she feels in Nsukka after her experiences in Enugu. Just as the skies open up, so does Kambili. Papa-Nnukwu says in chapter six that both the Catholic God and the Igbo Chukwu live in the sky. Kambili believes that weather is a way for God to communicate with the world and by persevering the scent of the sky, she is trying to hold on to God. She does not disturb the earthworms when she showers as she had before. There is a reverence for nature but also a peace with nature. Kambili is truly happy in this moment.

Kambili and Jaja's continuing coming of age can be gauged by their reactions to the news of Yewande Coker's daughter. After seeing her father killed by a mail bomb at their dining table, Yewande's daughter has not spoken a word. Papa has sent her to the best doctors to cure her, insisting it is God's work and not his own that is responsible. The benevolence Papa shows other people's children is a contrast to the punishment he metes out with his own. For both, God is responsible. In the case of Yewande's daughter, he does not take credit for a miracle – even though no miracle has occurred. And with his children, he is not to blame for their pain; he is saving them from hellfire. The same attitude that makes him humble absolves him of his guilt. Jaja does not think that God is responsible for her cure. Papa's money is responsible. Furthermore, he says she will never be healed. The psychological scars are permanent and though she speaks again, she will carry the emotional burden the rest of her life. Jaja is speaking of Yewande's daughter's pain, but also his own. Though he has healed from his beatings, the psychological impact remains.

Kambili, her faith intact, still believes that God is working through Papa's good deeds. She praises God for the girl's speech as she is starting to find her own. Her increasingly malleable faith allows her to ascribe her growth to grace. Kambili and Jaja no longer see eye to eye on this matter, but they can respect one another as individuals. In the long run, this is a better outcome than to be bound by unspoken misery. At Nsukka, Jaja refuses to speak to his father. Kambili refuses as well, though she is conflicted about it. Silence is a weapon that Jaja wields to punish Papa.

Summary and Analysis of Chapters Fifteen and Sixteen

Summary

Chapter Fifteen

Following the rains, a chill falls over Nsukka. Father Amadi dines with the family, chiding Amaka for not yet choosing a name for confirmation. She scans a list he has written up for her but still refuses to take an English name. He asks if she would be able, just this once, to accept the way things are done. Amaka doesn't understand why she can't choose an Igbo name, since she will not be called by her confirmation name. Aunty Ifeoma snaps at her daughter, telling her to just choose a name. Amaka does not agree, leaves the table, and blasts music from her room. The next day, Easter Sunday, Amaka does not join the other young people in the confirmation ceremony. Kambili reminisces about her own ceremony where she was named Ruth, her father's choice.

Aunty Ifeoma decides it is time to visit the miracle at Aokpe. Jaja does not want to go. Obiora stays home as well to look after Chima. Aunty Ifeoma asks Father Amadi to join the women. Amaka teases Kambili – he agrees to come for her. Hundreds of cars filled with Catholics on the pilgrimage to the apparition clog Aokpe. It is chaotic. A girl announces that she sees the Beautiful Woman, the Virgin Mary, in a tree. Others find her in the sun. Kambili watches the tree. It sways, depositing flame-colored petals on the ground. Ribbons cordoning off the apparition area shake though there is no wind. People around Kambili shake as well. The sun turns white and Kambili sees the Virgin everywhere – in the sun, on the back of her hand, in the smile of a man. On the ride home, Amaka says it doesn't matter if Our Lady appeared or not. The pilgrimage is the reason Kambili and Jaja came to Nsukka in the first place, so Aokpe will always be special. Kambili is the only one who sees the Blessed Virgin. Father Amadi, watching Kambili in the rearview mirror, says that something from God was happening there.

Kambili joins Father Amadi as he says goodbye to the families of Nsukka. Her throat eased by singing along with the Igbo songs of his car's radio, she tells him she loves him. Father Amadi presses his face to hers and tells her that she is beautiful and that she will have more love than she will need in a lifetime. She wants to kiss him and tell him that he is wrong. She cries on the way home. Aunty Ifeoma tells her to brighten up and to pray for her visa interview the next day. Kambili will not pray for what she does not want.

Kambili sits on the bed in Amaka's room, not saying anything about her day with Father Amadi. To Kambili's surprise, Amaka tells her she is singing along with her music. Amaka sighs. How will she find Fela tapes in America? Kambili does not know how to comfort her.

The children are waiting on the veranda when Aunty Ifeoma arrives home from her interview in Lagos. She tells them she got the visa. Obiora screams in excitement and Chima hugs his mother. Amaka, Kambili and Jaja do not rise. They have to move out of the flat in two weeks, then find enough money for the tickets. Aunty Ifeoma says they will go to Enugu with Kambili and Jaja to ask Papa to help. She will also convince Papa to send his children to boarding school. Finality hangs in the air, heavy and hollow.

Father Amadi's last day sneaks up on Kambili. She feels her new, fragile life will break into pieces. He asks her to spend a few hours with him before lunch, but she says no. She asks him if Aunty Ifeoma asked him to take her to the stadium the first time. He says yes, but that he wanted to take her everywhere after that. He tells her he will return in the evening, but she doesn't look up at him. Amaka comes out to comfort her and jokes that they will campaign against celibacy in the church when they go to university together. Kambili tells her to stop teasing. She knows Father Amadi will never leave the priesthood, even though she desperately wants him to. That night, she copies his German address into her notebook and he wipes away her tears. Father Amadi embraces Kambili. At dinner, she busies herself locking away the parts of her she will not need when he is gone.

Kambili stirs violently in her sleep, waking Amaka. Amaka holds her until the morning. Kambili does not tell Amaka about her dreams. She dreamt Father Amadi was chasing her through a rocky path littered with bruised allamanda plants. Father Amadi turned into Papa, dressed in a floor-length sack he wears on Ash Wednesday. Kambili is grateful for the sunlight the next morning.

After packing up the flat, the apartment looks eerily empty. Aunty Ifeoma decides they will take a farewell tour of Nsukka with the fuel they have left. They go to Odim Hill and, on impulse, climb up to picnic on the top. The view is wonderful. Obiora tells his sister she should paint the view. Instead of responding, Amaka takes off running to the top. Jaja and Chima follow. Aunty Ifeoma asks Kambili what she is waiting for, then takes off herself. Kambili runs after them, thinking of Father Amadi. She beats her aunt to the peak, then laughs easily when Ifeoma suggests she become a sprinter. When the sun turns red and is about to fall, they leave.

While they are playing cards in the living room, the phone rings. Aunty Ifeoma answers and then screams. Kambili makes out nwunye m in her cries and thinks something has happened to Mama. Kambili grabs the phone and her mother tells her that Papa is dead. They found him at the factory. Kambili, in shock, asks if it was a letter bomb. Jaja takes the phone and Aunty Ifeoma makes Kambili lie down. She stares at a sack of rice, lost in thoughts of her father. She did not think it was possible for her father to die.

Chapter Sixteen

At home, Kambili and Jaja stare at the place where the étagère used to be while Mama packs Papa's things. A violent rain starts to fall, pulling cashews and mangos off the trees. They would rot on the ground with the sickening sweetness. Mama has the gates of the compound locked to deter visits from guests. Even members from the umunna in Abba were turned away. Sisi serves drinks to the children in the same cups as Papa used to drink his tea. Jaja refuses. He shakes his head and declares that he should have taken care of Mama.

Kambili says the God works in mysterious ways. Jaja laughs. He asks her about Job and Jesus. Look at what God did to his faithful servant, and to His own Son? Mama receives a telephone call. There has been an autopsy and poison has been found. She had been poisoning Papa's tea since she came back from Nsukka. Jaja takes the blame for the crime and is arrested.

Analysis

Amaka and Kambili's faith are challenged in this chapter. Amaka, after much deliberation and stubbornness, decides to not take an English confirmation name. She does not participate in the ceremony. Like Jaja, she breaks from her faith. Amaka and Kambili visit the apparition in Aokpe. Kambili is the only one to see the Virgin Mary. She sees her in the tree, in the sun, and in the smile of every man. For Kambili, God is truly everywhere. As she realizes with Father Amadi, faith does not only occur in sanctified places. He speaks through nature and goodness, both more prosaic and more powerful than she imagined. Kambili's journey of her own faith comes to a close here. She will always be devout, but not in the way Papa is devout. She acknowledges faiths outside of her own, taking from them pieces that help her reconcile the world.

On their last day in Nsukka, Aunty Ifeoma takes the family to the top of Odim Hill. This is a holy place for the family. Kambili is prompted to run up after her cousins and, though she gets a late start, she bests many of them. Aunty Ifeoma tells her she should be a sprinter. This echoes what Father Amadi had said to her earlier. At the top of the hill, Kambili tries to find Father Amadi everywhere. As she surveys the beauty of the surroundings, she longs for the man she has fallen in love with. He has given her confidence enough to run up the hill and also to rise to adulthood. At the top, Obiora finds a grasshopper and proclaims how strong it is. Both he and Jaja are strong in their own ways.

Jaja knows about the murder before Kambili and the police do. It is unclear whether or not he had known what Mama was doing while it was happening, but he is complicit in the aftermath. When Kambili tells him that God works in mysterious ways, he turns a critical eye to the scriptures. He knows that Mama, not God, killed Papa. Unlike with Papa's refusal to be acknowledged for his deeds, Jaja knows someone must take the blame. He steps up and protects his mother, in his mind, to make up for the ways in which he has not protected her in the past. He has learned, from watching Obiora stand up to the soldiers and question authority, that manhood depends on strength and calls for familial loyalty. Jaja is now a man. He also can no longer reconcile his faith with what happens in the world. Unlike Kambili, he is unable to see anything but rigid interpretations as he has been taught. When he thinks of God as the father, he is as disappointed in Him as he is in Papa. Jaja ultimately rejects both fathers.

These chapters conclude the section entitled The Pieces of Gods. This can refer to the broken figurines, which leads to Jaja's broken faith and also the Achike family themselves. Each individual is a piece of the gods and the whole of the family is broken by Papa's death and Aunty Ifeoma's impending move to America. Kambili also feels that she is breaking into pieces because Father Amadi is leaving. There are both positive and negative connotations to this title. The whole of Kambili and her familial unit is being torn to pieces, but Kambili is also taking pieces of different gods to heart.

Summary and Analysis of Chapter Seventeen

PART FOUR – A DIFFERENT SILENCE: THE PRESENT

Summary

Nearly three years later, Kambili and Mama drive to the prison to visit Jaja. Mama has been reduced to skin and bones. After Jaja was arrested, she told people, including newspapers, that she was responsible for Papa's murder. But they did not believe her. Since then, she has been different. Out of pity, no one has criticized her for not attending the one- and two-year memorial masses for Papa. No one mentions that she has not cut her hair, which is customary for widows.

Each week Mama and Kambili visit Jaja. Usually, they go on separate days. But this day is different. Their lawyers, respected members of the state, have told the Achikes that Jaja will be released. Since the Head of State died atop a prostitute, his regime is being swept away. The lawyers and activists have placed the guilt for the murder on the regime. Like Ade Coker, they argue he was killed for his free speech. Almost 200 people imprisoned falsely are to be released. Jaja is fourth on the list.

But Kambili and Mama have not yet let themselves rejoice. A silence still falls over the house. They do not speak of how much money they have after half of Papa's estate went to the church in addition to donations he secretly made to several charities. Kambili tells their new driver to put her Fela tape on in the car.

Kambili reminisces about the last time she visited Nsukka. The lion statue no longer gleams and there is no longer power. She visits Aunty Ifeoma's flat, the bemused new tenants letting her in. Despite the changes, Kambili lets out a throaty laugh. Even though the town is in disrepair, the air smells of hills and history. Nsukka can let loose something in your soul, the sound emerging like a freedom song.

They arrive at the prison. Jaja is back in his old, overcrowded cell. He shares the cramped quarters with a number of men. The only bathroom is a plastic bag that they share. They fight over who gets to take it outside, because that person gets to see sunlight. Jaja had a better cell, equipped with a bed and books, because their lawyers knew the right people to bribe. But Jaja says he does not mind the mice and cockroaches, only sleeping next to another man's feces. Jaja is also beaten routinely for insubordination. Kambili is not sure if he does anything to provoke the abuse, or if it is just business as usual in the prison. Jaja won't say.

Jaja's official status this whole time has been Awaiting Trial. His shoulders, which bloomed in Nsukka, have sagged. In the letters Amaka has written to Kambili, she mentions her letters to the office of the Head of State and to the Nigerian embassy in America complaining about his treatment. But she does not tell Jaja this and Jaja does not write to Amaka. What will he say? Aunty Ifeoma sends him tape recordings of her family's voices.

As reported in Aunty Ifeoma's letters, she works two jobs. One at a small community college and the other at a pharmacy. Amaka says her family does not have time to laugh anymore and they barely see one another. She says that Chima "outfats" his outfits monthly. Obiora writes the cheeriest letters. On scholarship at a private school, he is encouraged rather than reported for challenging his teachers.

Mama and Kambili offer a bribe to the guard and are ushered in to see Jaja. When he comes out, Kambili takes a deep breath. New emotions are forming where the old ones are dissolving. She thinks about a letter from Father Amadi assuring her that Jaja will be released soon. The letter is in her bag – she always carries his letters in her bag until the next one arrives. Amaka teases her for being lovey-dovey, but there is nothing romantic in their letters. When she asks him if she is happy, he does not respond. She is not competing with God for his affections; she is sharing him with God.

Jaja's T-shirt, brought new by Kambili two weeks ago, is already filthy. There is a hardness in his eyes now. They eat quickly, Mama trembling at Kambili's side. They tell Jaja that he is being released. He responds that there are many interesting characters in his cell. Kambili corrects him – he is not being moved, but released from prison altogether. He says nothing. His eyes are too full of guilt to realize that Kambili thinks he is her hero. Though he often wishes he did more to protect his family, Kambili does not think he should have done more.

In this new silence, Kambili thinks about the old silence, when Papa was alive. She does not tell Jaja that she offers prayers for Papa every Sunday and that she longs to see him in her dreams. Sometimes she makes her own dreams, but even then she and Papa cannot meet. Their time is up and Jaja gets led away without making eye contact to his family.

When they leave the prison, there is a moment of hope. Kambili laughs and tells Mama that they will take Jaja to Nsukka and to America to see Aunty Ifeoma, then to Abba to plant new orange trees, and he will plant purple hibiscus again.

Analysis

The book closes on the present. It is nearly three years later and Jaja has been in prison for murdering Papa. As the title of this section suggests, there is a different silence in Enugu. Mama is silent now, wracked with grief. She has tried to tell everyone that she is to blame for the murder, but her confession has fallen on deaf ears. She speaks with Papa's money in the form of bribes for the prison guard and lawyers who participate in the corrupt system. They no longer speak out against the same system the Standard would criticize. In her home, Mama does not speak. Kambili respects her silence, knowing that, as before, some truths cannot be spoken.

Before, the silence was a necessity to maintain Papa's image. Now, the silence is self-preservation. Jaja no longer speaks with his eyes. Hardened by his brutal experiences in prison, he has learned to shut the vulnerable parts of himself away. He cannot take comfort in Kambili or else the house of cards he has built that enables him to live through prison will tumble down, like Mama's figurines. As Amaka understands, what can he say?

America is not the Eden that Obiora hopes it to be. Though he thrives in America, the rest of the family struggles in their new home. Aunty Ifeoma holds down two jobs to make ends meet and Amaka feels isolated from her roots. And though the Nsukka Kambili visits is devoid of the people who once made it a home, Kambili still seeks refuge there. Odim Hill still stands, the air scented with hills and history. It is the history of her country and Kambili's own history. Rather than her own home, Nsukka's transformative power is Kambili's refuge. She comes here to restore herself, to free the song within her that is forced into silence in Enugu. Kambili has roots now. She listens to Fela's tapes and reminisces about Amaka, but the music has also become her own.

Summary and Analysis of Chapter Seventeen

Suggested Essay Questions

1. What does the purple hibiscus represent?

   Aunty Ifeoma grows the purple hibiscus, a rare hybrid created by a botanist friend of hers. Jaja is drawn to the flowers when he arrives in Nsukka. For Jaja, the flowers represent freedom. Instead of just following what must be, Aunty Ifeoma's purple hibiscus are both uniquely beautiful and a new creation. They are a symbol of an alternative to the rigid life that has been created for him and his sister. When he takes the stalks to his home, he brings with them a new sense of self and possibility.

2. Kambili describes in detail many different aspects of nature, including plants, insects and weather. How does the environment relate to the narrative?

   The environment is used to reflect both inner turmoil and joy. When Ade Coker dies, a heavy rain falls. Likewise, sadness and pressure fall on Papa. After Papa throws the missal, a strong wind uproots the frangipani trees and the satellite dish. When Kambili begins to mature, her relationship with the natural world also changes. Instead of being frightened by earthworms in Aunty Ifeoma's bath, she lets them be. Kambili's comfort with nature is directly related to her ease of self.

3. Papa uses Igbo and English at different times. Discuss what this signifies about his character.

   Though raised by an Igbo traditionalist, Papa rarely uses his native tongue at home and never in public. Papa was schooled by missionaries in Nigeria and in England and is educated in colonial ways. For him, his accent belies his prominence. He speaks with an English-inflected accent to both Father Benedict and Mother Lucy. Maintaining an image of an African who is comfortable with European ways helps to cement his standing in the community. He uses this stature to help his friend Ade. But Papa also carries a shame for his roots. His voice communicates both his education and also his separation from his ancestral traditions.

4. Compare the relationship between Amaka and Obiora to the relationship between Kambili and Jaja.

   Amaka and Obiora are siblings who share passions but also don't see eye to eye on important topics. Both children are intellectually curious and argumentative. They have been raised to question authority. However, Amaka is fiercely loyal to Nigeria and Obiora finds new hope in the dream of America. Unlike Kambili and Jaja, Amaka and Obiora are not scared to disagree. Kambili and Jaja are united by silence. When Jaja begins to spread his wings a bit, Kambili is dismayed that she can no longer communicate with him via the secret language of their eyes. Ultimately, both Amaka and

Obiora and Kambili and Jaja allow each other to nurture separate identities but still love one another.

5. Kambili describes in detail several dreams. Why are they important?

Kambili's dreams are clues to how she feels about certain people and events. Since Kambili only rarely speaks her mind, her mind speaks for her. She dreams that she has Aunty Ifeoma's laugh because she wishes she could talk as freely and energetically like her aunt. When Amaka is deriding her, Kambili dreams her cousin is flushing her down the toilet. Kambili's dreams are a gateway into her mind.

6. Purple Hibiscus charts the coming of age of both Kambili and Jaja. Discuss how each Achike sibling matures over the course of the novel.

Kambili is characterized by her lack of voice. She stutters and coughs and can barely rise above a whisper. Both she and Jaja are sheltered and intimidated by her father. Both children, as they mature into adults, must overcome their father. While Jaja's rebellions are more overt – missing communion, asking for his room key, taking the blame for his mother's crime – Kambili's are more personal. She does not reject her faith and compassion, but rather adapts them to fit her new, more complex, worldview. Through all of their hardships, Jaja remains Kambili's hero.

7. Religion is a crucial theme in Purple Hibiscus. Discuss how religion influences the characters.

There are two religions that are prominently featured in Purple Hibiscus: Catholicism and traditional Igbo practice Papa can be viewed as a symbol of fundamentalism in Nigeria. Influenced by his colonial education, Papa eradicates all traces of his traditional past and indoctrinates his children into religion as it was preached to him. God seeks perfection and Papa's way to instill perfection is to punish failure. Papa does not let his children spend much time with his own father for he is a "heathen." Papa's prejudice severs his ties with his ancestry. However, as Kambili realizes, there are similarities between the faiths of Papa and Papa-Nnukwu. Aunty Ifeoma and, later, Kambili, honor both faiths in their more modernized take on devotion.

8. Why does Mama poison Papa?

Mama's murder of Papa is first and foremost to protect herself and her children from his abuse. However, she poisons him because she feels she has no other option. She dismisses Aunty Ifeoma's advice to leave her home as "university talk." After losing another child at his hands, however, Mama realizes that something must be done. In an environment of repression and violence, she fights back using the only method available to her – poison.

9. Discuss how the political unrest in Nigeria affects the Achike family.

Though the political unrest is removed from Kambili's day to day life, corruption touches her family. Papa's friend and fellow pro-democracy activist Ade Coker is murdered in front of his family. Papa is distraught when this happens and remarks that Nigeria is in decline. The escalating violence and police presence echo the rising tensions inside the Achike home. Kambili and Jaja's fight for independence echoes the fight of the pro-democracy activists.

10. Discuss the significance of Kambili's crush on Father Amadi.

The comforting presence of Father Amadi causes two changes in Kambili's life. Her physical attraction to Father Amadi expedites her steps towards womanhood. Father Amadi also greatly influences Kambili's shifting paradigm of faith. He tells her he did not have a calling, but rather that the priesthood was able to answer the most questions. Father Amadi also incorporates Igbo song and prayer into his sermons. Kambili realizes that her faith and ancestral traditions do not have to be mutually exclusive. She is able to forge her identity as both a sexual woman and as more liberal Catholic.

Colonialism, Independence and Corruption

The first line of the novel includes an allusion to Chinua Achebe's masterpiece *Things Fall Apart*. One of the first prominent English-language Nigerian novels, *Things Fall Apart* chronicles an Igbo man's rise and fall in a village beset by European missionaries. In that novel, the fictionalized tensions between the missionaries and the clan represent the clash between old and new ways. The goal of the missionaries is to convert the Nigerians to Christianity. While a portion of missionaries intended to preach their gospel while respecting the indigenous cultures, others used their righteousness as justification for oppressing and even enslaving Nigerians.

The presence of the white people in Nigeria had political, economic and religious implications. Clan rulers who were not amenable to the British were replaced with those that would cooperate. This type of corruption continued into the post-colonial era where those in power would reward their allies and oppress those who dissent.

The colonial period lasted from 1850 through 1929, when nationalist movements gained in popularity. In 1960, Nigeria gained independence from Britain. But this independence ushered in a wave of instability culminating in a civil war. Bloody military coups displaced those in power. The Igbo people created their own state, the Republic of Biafra, and declared independence in 1967. For thirty months, 1 to 3 million people died in the civil war between the Nigerians and the Biafrans.

In the 1970s and 1980s, oil dictated politics. The boom of oil production again ushered in a political system that was dictated by profit. Another wave of military coups led to instability and corruption. For example, in 1993, General Sani Abacha took power and staved off overthrow by bribing the military. As the Head of State Big Oga in *Purple Hibiscus*, Abacha dies under unusual circumstances. Hundreds of millions of dollars were found in secret accounts. The military finally returned the country to democracy in the 1999, although those elections were widely perceived to be unfree and unfair.

Several key political figures are either mentioned or fictionalized in Purple Hibiscus.

Adichie has acknowledged that Ade Coker's life and death are nods to both Dele Giwa, murdered journalist, and Ken Saro-Wiwa. Saro-Wiwa was a poet and author who protested on behalf of the Ogoni People against the environmental ruin of their ancestral home caused by massive oil drilling. Saro-Wiwa was an outspoken critic against the government and was arrested and hanged under Abacha's rule.

Amaka's beloved Fela Ransome Kuti is one of the best-known Nigerian musicians. Like Papa, Kuti was educated in England. Kuti created Afrobeat, a style of music that blends jazz with traditional African rhythms. He railed against the colonial mentality of his upbringing and advocated for both a return to traditions and democracy. He was arrested, beaten and tortured several times for openly criticizing the government. The popularity of his music was seen as a threat to the military establishment.

Author of ClassicNote and Sources

Christine McKeever, author of ClassicNote. Completed on August 07, 2011, copyright held by GradeSaver.

Updated and revised Elizabeth Weinbloom May 12, 2012. Copyright held by GradeSaver.

Falola, Toyin and Matthew M. Heaton. A History of Nigeria. Cambridge: Cambridge University Press, 2008.

Veal, Michael E.. Fela: The Life and Times of an African Musical Icon. Philadelphia: Temple University Press, 2000.

Daria Tunca. "The Chimamande Ngozi Adichie Website." 2004-10-15. 2011-08-04. <http://www.l3.ulg.ac.be/adichie/index.html>.

"Nigerian Identity is Burdensome: The Chimamande Ngozi Adichie Interview." Wale Adebanwi. 2005-11-10. 2011-08-02. <http://nigeriavillagesquare.com/forum/books-creative-writing/48192-nigerian-identity-burden

"Chimamanda Ngozi Adichie: How the acclaimed novelist is becoming a role-model and mentor." Katy Guest. 2009-04-10. 2011-08-02. <http://www.independent.co.uk/arts-entertainment/books/features/chimamanda-ngozi-adichie

"The Punch: Dele Giwa, 24 years after." Samuel Awoyinfa. 2010-10-17. 2011-08-05. <http://www.punchng.com/Articl.aspx?theartic=Art201010171165479>.

Quiz 1

1. **What type of figurines does Mama collect?**
    A. saints
    B. flowers
    C. ballerinas
    D. birds

2. **What typed of juice does Papa offer to his family on Palm Sunday**
    A. cashew
    B. orange
    C. pineapple
    D. mango

3. **When Papa drinks tea, what does he offer his children?**
    A. biscuits
    B. love sips
    C. milk
    D. their own cup of tea

4. **What color are Mama's hibiscus flowers?**
    A. purple
    B. yellow
    C. red
    D. blue

5. **Why does Papa throw his missal at Jaja?**
    A. Jaja skips communion
    B. Jaja failed a test
    C. Jaja breaks one of Mama's figurine
    D. Jaja ran away

6. **What is the name of the Achike family's church?**
    A. St. Paul
    B. St. Agnes
    C. St Beatrice
    D. St. John

7. **When Mama brings in Kambili's school uniform, what does she tell her?**
    A. Dinner is ready
    B. She is pregnant
    C. She is ill
    D. She is leaving Papa

8. **Jaja was awarded _____ in school?**
    A. Valedictorian
    B. Neatest Boy
    C. Most Prompt
    D. Best Dressed

9. **What is NOT included on the schedules Papa prepares for his children?**
    A. Prayer
    B. TV
    C. Study Time
    D. Family Time

10. **What is the name of Papa's newspaper?**
    A. The Bugle
    B. The Punch
    C. The Times
    D. The Standard

11. **What is Ade Coker's job?**
    A. Editor
    B. Priest
    C. Foreman
    D. Professor

12. **How do Kambili and Jaja secretly communicate?**
    A. Through notes
    B. With their eyes
    C. In hand gestures
    D. in morse code

13. **Which of these is a symbol of sympathy with the protesters?**
    A. Green branches
    B. Red flower
    C. White dove
    D. Yellow sun

14. **Whose portrait hangs in the Achike dining room?**
    A. The Pope
    B. Father Benedict
    C. Papa's father, Papa-Nnukwu
    D. Mama's father, Grandfather

15. **How does Mama console herself when she loses her child?**
    A. By cooking
    B. By singing
    C. By going for a drive
    D. By cleaning the figurines

16. **When Kambili places second at school, who places first?**
    A. Ezinne
    B. Chinwe Yideze
    C. Jaja
    D. Amaka

17. **Why does Mama take the kids to the market to buy?**
    A. Bags and sandals
    B. School supplies
    C. New clothes
    D. Fruit

18. **What does Mother Lucy ask Kambili to lead at school?**
    A. Prayer
    B. A parade
    C. The Pledge
    D. A sing-a-long

19. **Why do Kambili's classmates call her backyard snob?**
    A. She is wealthy
    B. She does not speak
    C. She runs straight to her car after class
    D. All of the above

20. **Who narrates the novel?**
    A. Kambili
    B. Jaja
    C. Mama
    D. Papa

21. **What is Aunty Ifeoma's profession?**
    A. Artist
    B. Writer
    C. Professor
    D. Accountant

22. **At the start of the novel, how old is Kambili?**
    A. 13
    B. 15
    C. 18
    D. 20

23. **The first part of the book takes place during which religious holiday?**
    A. Easter
    B. Christmas
    C. Palm Sunday
    D. The Epiphany

24. **Who is Papa-Nnukwu?**
    A. Mama's grandfather
    B. Papa's grandfather
    C. Mama's father
    D. Papa's father

25. **How long does Papa allow the children to stay at Papa-Nnukwu's house?**
    A. 2 hours
    B. 30 minutes
    C. 15 minutes
    D. 1 hour

Quiz 1 Answer Key

1. **(C)** ballerinas
2. **(A)** cashew
3. **(B)** love sips
4. **(C)** red
5. **(A)** Jaja skips communion
6. **(B)** St. Agnes
7. **(B)** She is pregnant
8. **(B)** Neatest Boy
9. **(B)** TV
10. **(D)** The Standard
11. **(A)** Editor
12. **(B)** With their eyes
13. **(A)** Green branches
14. **(D)** Mama's father, Grandfather
15. **(D)** By cleaning the figurines
16. **(B)** Chinwe Yideze
17. **(A)** Bags and sandals
18. **(C)** The Pledge
19. **(D)** All of the above
20. **(A)** Kambili
21. **(C)** Professor
22. **(B)** 15
23. **(C)** Palm Sunday
24. **(D)** Papa's father
25. **(C)** 15 minutes

Quiz 2

1. **What is the currency of Nigeria called?**
   A. Dollar
   B. Lire
   C. Naira
   D. Pound

2. **How many children does Aunty Ifeoma have?**
   A. 1
   B. 2
   C. 3
   D. 4

3. **What does Amaka want to do when she arrives at the Achike house?**
   A. Watch TV
   B. Listen to music
   C. Dance
   D. Plait Kambili's hair

4. **Where does Aunty Ifeoma take Kambili and Jaja at Christmas?**
   A. A traditionalist festival
   B. Shopping
   C. To their home
   D. To the market

5. **What does Mama want to give Aunty Ifeoma?**
   A. A dress
   B. Gas cylinders
   C. A TV
   D. A book

6. **What are mmuo?**
   A. snacks
   B. drinks
   C. animals
   D. spirits

7. **At the start of the novel, how old is Jaja?**
    A. 12
    B. 15
    C. 17
    D. 20

8. **Why does Papa hit Kambili for eating cornflakes?**
    A. She takes finishes the milk
    B. She eats the last bowl
    C. He was going to cook breakfast
    D. She breaks a fast

9. **When her family confesses, when does Kambili take her turn?**
    A. second
    B. last
    C. third
    D. first

10. **Why does Papa agree to send his kids to Nsukka?**
    A. To study with their cousins
    B. To see Papa-Nnukwu
    C. To help their aunt
    D. To see the miracle at Aokpe

11. **What is the shape of the statue in front of the University in Nsukka?**
    A. Man
    B. Bear
    C. Lion
    D. Tiger

12. **What is "To Restore the Dignity of Man"?**
    A. The University's motto
    B. A song Amaka sings
    C. A book Obiora reads
    D. A poem Aunty Ifeoma writes

13. **Where does Jaja sleep in Aunty Ifeoma's flat?**
    A. In Amaka's room
    B. In the kitchen
    C. On the verandah
    D. In the living room

14. **What is Amaka's favorite possession?**
    A. A blouse
    B. A tape recorder
    C. A comb
    D. A book

15. **Why do the students of the University riot?**
    A. They have failed their exams
    B. They want a holiday
    C. They want new dorms
    D. They have no water or power

16. **What does Kambili help Amaka peel?**
    A. Apples
    B. Cassava
    C. Potatoes
    D. Yams

17. **Why does Aunty Ifeoma want to go to Aokpe?**
    A. She was born there
    B. There is a good bookstore
    C. There is a nice restaurant
    D. There is a miraculous apparition

18. **What is Jaja's real name?**
    A. Obiora
    B. Chukwuku
    C. Ifeodiora
    D. Chima

19. **Aunty Ifeoma refers to Jaja of Opobo, who is known as _____?**
   A. The First King
   B. The Honest King
   C. The Defiant King
   D. The Timid King

20. **Which child wears eyeglasses?**
   A. Obiora
   B. Kambili
   C. Jaja
   D. Amaka

21. **Where does Father Amadi take Kambili when they go out the first time?**
   A. Church
   B. School
   C. Stadium
   D. Park

22. **Why does Papa-Nnukwu come to stay with Aunty Ifeoma?**
   A. His house burns down
   B. He is ill
   C. He wants to see Kambili and Jaja
   D. It is his birthday

23. **What does Amaka think her cousins are?**
   A. Abnormal
   B. Friendly
   C. Fun
   D. Happy

24. **What does Amaka do when Kambili finally talks back to her?**
   A. Smiles
   B. Hits her
   C. Storms off
   D. Yells

25. **Why does Aunty Ifeoma wake Kambili up at dawn?**
    A. To go to school
    B. To make breakfast
    C. To get water
    D. To watch Papa-Nnukwu's innocence ritual

Quiz 2 Answer Key

1. **(C)** Naira
2. **(C)** 3
3. **(A)** Watch TV
4. **(A)** A traditionalist festival
5. **(B)** Gas cylinders
6. **(D)** spirits
7. **(C)** 17
8. **(D)** She breaks a fast
9. **(D)** first
10. **(D)** To see the miracle at Aokpe
11. **(C)** Lion
12. **(A)** The University's motto
13. **(D)** In the living room
14. **(B)** A tape recorder
15. **(D)** They have no water or power
16. **(D)** Yams
17. **(D)** There is a miraculous apparition
18. **(B)** Chukwuku
19. **(C)** The Defiant King
20. **(A)** Obiora
21. **(C)** Stadium
22. **(B)** He is ill
23. **(A)** Abnormal
24. **(A)** Smiles
25. **(D)** To watch Papa-Nnukwu's innocence ritual

Quiz 3

1. **What is the red stain that appears on Kambili's hand when she chases Father Amadi?**
   A. Lipstick
   B. Blood
   C. Paint
   D. Juice

2. **What does Amaka give Kambili when she returns to Enugu?**
   A. A book of poetry
   B. A pair of shorts
   C. A painting of Papa-Nnukwu
   D. A tube of lipstick

3. **Why does Papa pour hot water over his children's feet?**
   A. Because they share a home with Papa-Nnukwu
   B. Because they are late
   C. Because they break Mama's figurines
   D. Because they cut school

4. **What does Jaja bring home from Nsukka?**
   A. A chicken
   B. Purple hibiscus
   C. A book
   D. A soccer ball

5. **What was Amaka's confirmation name?**
   A. Frances
   B. Mary
   C. Ruth
   D. Agnes

6. **How does Ade Coker die?**
   A. Illness
   B. Mail bomb
   C. He is shot
   D. Car accident

7. **What do the soldiers take to Papa's factory?**
   A. Snakes
   B. Torches
   C. Rats
   D. Bribes

8. **Why does Papa kick Kambili?**
   A. She hides at Papa-Nnukwu's painting
   B. She tries to run away
   C. She cheats on a test
   D. She talks back to him

9. **What swarms at Aunty Ifeoma's flat?**
   A. Cicadas
   B. Aku
   C. Bees
   D. Flies

10. **What does Kambili find in Aunty Ifeoma's shower?**
    A. A snail
    B. A beetle
    C. A lizard
    D. An earthworm

11. **Who is Mama Joe?**
    A. The woman who plaits Kambili's hair
    B. Aunty Ifeoma's mother
    C. A neighbor
    D. A professor

12. **When Kambili is getting her hair plaited, what is in the bucket next to her?**
    A. Mangos
    B. Snails
    C. Aku
    D. Earthworms

13. **Which of these is NOT a type of food?**
   A. Okpa
   B. Fufu
   C. Mmuo
   D. Moi Moi

14. **Where does Father Amadi get assigned?**
   A. America
   B. England
   C. Germany
   D. France

15. **Why does the University get shut down?**
   A. It gets flooded
   B. The students riot
   C. It is deemed unsafe
   D. It burns down

16. **Who kills the chicken brought to Aunty Ifeoma?**
   A. Obiora
   B. Jaja
   C. Amaka
   D. Chima

17. **What happens when the soldiers barge in on Aunty Ifeoma's flat?**
   A. They ransack the flat
   B. She is arrested
   C. Amaka is arrested
   D. Obiora is arrested

18. **Where does Aunty Ifeoma decide to move?**
   A. America
   B. Germany
   C. Zimbabwe
   D. South Africa

19. **Why does Mama show up at Aunty Ifeoma's flat?**
    A. To plait Kambili's hair
    B. To bring Jaja books
    C. To go to Aokpe
    D. She was beaten again

20. **Who interrupts the conversation Aunty Ifeoma has with Chiaku?**
    A. Obiora
    B. Jaja
    C. Amaka
    D. Chima

21. **Amaka calls Kambili ne nwanne m nwanyi. What does it mean?**
    A. Cousin
    B. My friend
    C. My sister
    D. Enemy

22. **What does father slip off of Kambili's fingers?**
    A. Gloves
    B. Flower petals
    C. A bracelet
    D. A ring

23. **What comes "tumbling down" after Palm Sunday?**
    A. Mama's figurines
    B. Frangipani trees
    C. The satellite dish
    D. All of the above

24. **Why does Papa send Yewande Coker's daughter to the doctor?**
    A. She has a cough
    B. She has a fever
    C. She does not speak
    D. She has a sore throat

25. What does Jaja ask his father for when they return from Nsukka?

A. A TV for his room

B. The key to his room

C. New clothes

D. A Bible

Quiz 3 Answer Key

1. **(A)** Lipstick
2. **(C)** A painting of Papa-Nnukwu
3. **(A)** Because they share a home with Papa-Nnukwu
4. **(B)** Purple hibiscus
5. **(C)** Ruth
6. **(B)** Mail bomb
7. **(C)** Rats
8. **(A)** She hides at Papa-Nnukwu's painting
9. **(B)** Aku
10. **(D)** An earthworm
11. **(A)** The woman who plaits Kambili's hair
12. **(B)** Snails
13. **(C)** Mmuo
14. **(C)** Germany
15. **(B)** The students riot
16. **(B)** Jaja
17. **(A)** They ransack the flat
18. **(A)** America
19. **(D)** She was beaten again
20. **(A)** Obiora
21. **(C)** My sister
22. **(B)** Flower petals
23. **(D)** All of the above
24. **(C)** She does not speak
25. **(B)** The key to his room

Quiz 4

1. **What does Jaja use to barricade his door from Papa?**
   A. His desk
   B. A bookcase
   C. His dresser
   D. His bed

2. **How much time elapses between the final two chapters?**
   A. 3 months
   B. 3 days
   C. 3 weeks
   D. 3 years

3. **Aunty Ifeoma tells Kambili that the "angry" sun warns of what?**
   A. Drought
   B. Hurricane
   C. Rain
   D. Winds

4. **Why doesn't Kambili heat the rainwater?**
   A. To keep it cold
   B. To retain the scent of the sky
   C. It has already been heated
   D. She will cook with it later

5. **Where does Kambili see the apparition at Aokpe?**
   A. In a man's smile
   B. On her hand
   C. In the tree
   D. All of the above

6. **Why does Amaka say that Aokpe will always be special?**
   A. Because her father is buried there
   B. Because it brought Kambili and Jaja to Nsukka
   C. Because Aunty Ifeoma got married there
   D. Because Amaka saw the apparition

7. **How does Papa die?**
   A. He is poisoned
   B. Illness
   C. He is shot
   D. Car accident

8. **What does Obiora suggest they do at Odim Hill?**
   A. Run
   B. Sing
   C. Play
   D. Dance

9. **What does Aunty Ifeoma suggest Kambili become?**
   A. A lawyer
   B. An artist
   C. A sprinter
   D. A professor

10. **Kambili dreams two people chase her down a rocky path. Who?**
    A. Amaka and Aunty Ifeoma
    B. Obiora and Chima
    C. Jaja and Mama
    D. Papa and Father Amadi

11. **What do the lawyers bring Mama and Kambili when they say Jaja can be released?**
    A. Dinner
    B. Sweets
    C. Flowers
    D. Champagne

12. **What are the children doing at Aunty Ifeoma's when they find out Papa has died?**
    A. Playing cards
    B. Playing chess
    C. Drawing
    D. Watching TV

13. **What does Kambili stare at when she finds out Papa has died?**
    A. Jaja
    B. The TV
    C. A sack of rice
    D. A line of ants

14. **In the last chapter, why do the lawyers think they can get Jaja released?**
    A. There is new evidence
    B. The Head of State has died
    C. Jaja behaves well
    D. Mama has confessed

15. **What does Kambili listen to on the way to the prison?**
    A. A tape of Aunty Ifeoma's voice
    B. English prayers
    C. Igbo songs
    D. Fela

16. **What does Aunty Ifeoma send to Jaja in prison?**
    A. Tapes of her family's voices
    B. Clothes
    C. Magazines
    D. Cigarettes

17. **Mama and Kambili bribe the prison guard when they visit Jaja. How is the bribe concealed?**
    A. In a scarf
    B. In a magazine
    C. In a canister of food
    D. In a bag

18. **Where does Kambili want to take Jaja when he is released?**
    A. Nsukka
    B. America
    C. Abba
    D. All of the above

19. **What does Mama give Sisi when she gets married?**
    A. A dress
    B. A frangipani tree
    C. A car
    D. Sets of china

20. **One of Jaja's fingers is deformed. How was it injured?**
    A. It happened when he was born
    B. He slammed in a car door
    C. Papa punished him
    D. He sliced it while cooking

21. **Who gives the poison to Mama?**
    A. Sisi
    B. Amaka
    C. Kevin
    D. Aunty Ifeoma?

22. **Kambili dreams that Papa is pouring hot water over someone's feet. Whose?**
    A. Mama
    B. Amaka
    C. Father Amadi
    D. Aunty Ifeoma

23. **What does Kambili want to plant in Abba when Jaja is released?**
    A. Purple hibiscus
    B. Ixora
    C. Red hibiscus
    D. Orange trees

24. **Kambili says the air in Nsukka smells of hills and _____?**
    A. Freedom
    B. History
    C. Love
    D. Earth

25. Who has a dagger-shaped scar on his neck?

    A. Ade Coker

    B. Father Benedict

    C. Papa

    D. Kevin

Quiz 4 Answer Key

1. **(A)** His desk
2. **(D)** 3 years
3. **(C)** Rain
4. **(B)** To retain the scent of the sky
5. **(D)** All of the above
6. **(B)** Because it brought Kambili and Jaja to Nsukka
7. **(A)** He is poisoned
8. **(A)** Run
9. **(C)** A sprinter
10. **(D)** Papa and Father Amadi
11. **(D)** Champagne
12. **(A)** Playing cards
13. **(C)** A sack of rice
14. **(B)** The Head of State has died
15. **(D)** Fela
16. **(A)** Tapes of her family's voices
17. **(B)** In a magazine
18. **(D)** All of the above
19. **(D)** Sets of china
20. **(C)** Papa punished him
21. **(A)** Sisi
22. **(D)** Aunty Ifeoma
23. **(D)** Orange trees
24. **(B)** History
25. **(D)** Kevin

ClassicNotes

GrAdeSaver™

Getting you the grade since 1999™

Other ClassicNotes from GradeSaver™

12 Angry Men
1984
A&P and Other Stories
Absalom, Absalom
Adam Bede
The Adventures of Augie March
The Adventures of Huckleberry Finn
The Adventures of Tom Sawyer
The Aeneid
Agamemnon
The Age of Innocence
The Alchemist (Coelho)
The Alchemist (Jonson)
Alice in Wonderland
All My Sons
All Quiet on the Western Front
All the King's Men
All the Pretty Horses
Allen Ginsberg's Poetry
The Ambassadors
American Beauty
And Then There Were None
Angela's Ashes
Animal Farm
Anna Karenina
Anthem
Antigone
Antony and Cleopatra
Aristotle's Poetics
Aristotle's Politics

Aristotle: Nicomachean Ethics
As I Lay Dying
As You Like It
Astrophil and Stella
Atlas Shrugged
Atonement
The Awakening
Babbitt
The Bacchae
Bartleby the Scrivener
The Bean Trees
The Bell Jar
Beloved
Benito Cereno
Beowulf
Bhagavad-Gita
Billy Budd
Black Boy
Bleak House
Bless Me, Ultima
Blindness
Blood Wedding
The Bloody Chamber
Bluest Eye
The Bonfire of the Vanities
The Book of Daniel
The Book of the Duchess and Other Poems
The Book Thief
Brave New World
Breakfast at Tiffany's
Breakfast of Champions
The Brief Wondrous Life of Oscar Wao

The Brothers Karamazov
The Burning Plain and Other Stories
A Burnt-Out Case
By Night in Chile
Call of the Wild
Candide
The Canterbury Tales
Cat on a Hot Tin Roof
Cat's Cradle
Catch-22
The Catcher in the Rye
Cathedral
The Caucasian Chalk Circle
Charlotte Temple
Charlotte's Web
The Cherry Orchard
The Chocolate War
The Chosen
A Christmas Carol
Christopher Marlowe's Poems
Chronicle of a Death Foretold
Civil Disobedience
Civilization and Its Discontents
A Clockwork Orange
Coleridge's Poems
The Color of Water
The Color Purple
Comedy of Errors
Communist Manifesto
A Confederacy of Dunces

For our full list of over 250 Study Guides, Quizzes,
Sample College Application Essays, Literature Essays and E-texts, visit:

www.gradesaver.com

ClassicNotes

GrAdeSaver™

Getting you the grade since 1999™

For our full list of over 250 Study Guides, Quizzes,
Sample College Application Essays, Literature Essays and E-texts, visit:

www.gradesaver.com

ClassicNotes

GrΛdeSaver™

Getting you the grade since 1999™

Other ClassicNotes from GradeSaver™

Homo Faber
House of Mirth
The House of the Seven
    Gables
The House of the Spirits
House on Mango Street
How the Garcia Girls
    Lost Their Accents
Howards End
A Hunger Artist
The Hunger Games
I Know Why the Caged
    Bird Sings
I, Claudius
An Ideal Husband
Iliad
The Importance of Being
    Earnest
In Cold Blood
In Our Time
In the Time of the
    Butterflies
Inherit the Wind
An Inspector Calls
Interpreter of Maladies
Into the Wild
Invisible Man
The Island of Dr. Moreau
Jane Eyre
Jazz
The Jew of Malta
Johnny Tremain
Joseph Andrews
The Joy Luck Club
Julius Caesar
The Jungle

Jungle of Cities
Kama Sutra
Kate Chopin's Short
    Stories
Kidnapped
King Lear
King Solomon's Mines
The Kite Runner
The Lais of Marie de
    France
Last of the Mohicans
Leaves of Grass
The Legend of Sleepy
    Hollow
A Lesson Before Dying
Leviathan
Libation Bearers
Life is Beautiful
Life of Pi
Light In August
Like Water for Chocolate
The Lion, the Witch and
    the Wardrobe
Little Women
Lolita
Long Day's Journey Into
    Night
A Long Way Gone
Look Back in Anger
Lord Byron's Poems
Lord Jim
Lord of the Flies
The Lord of the Rings:
    The Fellowship of the
    Ring

The Lord of the Rings:
    The Return of the
    King
The Lord of the Rings:
    The Two Towers
A Lost Lady
The Lottery and Other
    Stories
Love in the Time of
    Cholera
The Love Song of J.
    Alfred Prufrock
The Lovely Bones
Lucy
Macbeth
Madame Bovary
Maestro
Maggie: A Girl of the
    Streets and Other
    Stories
Manhattan Transfer
Mankind: Medieval
    Morality Plays
Mansfield Park
The Marrow of Tradition
The Master and
    Margarita
MAUS
The Mayor of
    Casterbridge
Measure for Measure
Medea
Merchant of Venice
Metamorphoses
The Metamorphosis
Middlemarch

For our full list of over 250 Study Guides, Quizzes,
Sample College Application Essays, Literature Essays and E-texts, visit:

www.gradesaver.com

ClassicNotes

Gr\AdeSaver™

Getting you the grade since 1999™

Other ClassicNotes from GradeSaver™

Roll of Thunder, Hear My Cry
Romeo and Juliet
A Room of One's Own
A Room With a View
A Rose For Emily and Other Short Stories
Rosencrantz and Guildenstern Are Dead
Salome
The Scarlet Letter
The Scarlet Pimpernel
The Seagull
Season of Migration to the North
Second Treatise of Government
The Secret Life of Bees
The Secret River
Secret Sharer
Sense and Sensibility
A Separate Peace
Shakespeare's Sonnets
Shantaram
She Stoops to Conquer
Short Stories of Ernest Hemingway
Short Stories of F. Scott Fitzgerald
Siddhartha
Silas Marner
Sir Gawain and the Green Knight
Sir Thomas Wyatt: Poems

Sister Carrie
Six Characters in Search of an Author
Slaughterhouse Five
Snow Falling on Cedars
The Social Contract
Something Wicked This Way Comes
Song of Roland
Song of Solomon
Songs of Innocence and of Experience
Sons and Lovers
The Sorrows of Young Werther
The Sound and the Fury
The Sound of Waves
The Spanish Tragedy
Spenser's Amoretti and Epithalamion
Spring Awakening
The Stranger
A Streetcar Named Desire
A Study in Scarlet
Sula
The Sun Also Rises
Sundiata: An Epic of Old Mali
Tale of Two Cities
The Taming of the Shrew
The Tempest
Tender is the Night
Tess of the D'Urbervilles
Their Eyes Were Watching God

Things Fall Apart
The Things They Carried
A Thousand Splendid Suns
The Threepenny Opera
Through the Looking Glass
Thus Spoke Zarathustra
The Time Machine
Titus Andronicus
To Build a Fire
To Kill a Mockingbird
To the Lighthouse
The Tortilla Curtain
Touching Spirit Bear
Treasure Island
Trifles
Troilus and Cressida
Tropic of Cancer
Tropic of Capricorn
Tuesdays With Morrie
The Turn of the Screw
Twelfth Night
Twilight
Ulysses
Uncle Tom's Cabin
Utopia
Vanity Fair
A Very Old Man With Enormous Wings
Villette
A Vindication of the Rights of Woman
The Visit
Volpone
Waiting for Godot

For our full list of over 250 Study Guides, Quizzes,
Sample College Application Essays, Literature Essays and E-texts, visit:

www.gradesaver.com

ClassicNotes

Getting you the grade since 1999™

Other ClassicNotes from GradeSaver™

Waiting for Lefty
Walden
Washington Square
The Waste Land
The Wave
The Wealth of Nations
Where the Red Fern
    Grows
White Fang
A White Heron and
    Other Stories
White Noise
White Teeth
Who's Afraid of Virginia
    Woolf
Wide Sargasso Sea
Wieland
Winesburg, Ohio
The Winter's Tale
The Woman Warrior
Wordsworth's Poetical
    Works
Woyzeck
A Wrinkle in Time
Wuthering Heights
The Yellow Wallpaper
Yonnondio: From the
    Thirties
Zeitoun

For our full list of over 250 Study Guides, Quizzes,
Sample College Application Essays, Literature Essays and E-texts, visit:

www.gradesaver.com